DINOSAURS

What's Inside

- 4 What are dinosaurs?
- 6 Kinds of dinosaurs
- 8 The Triassic period: 252-201 million years ago
- 10 The Jurassic period: 201-145 million years ago
- 12 The Cretaceous period: 145-66 million years ago
- 14 Where are they now?
- 16 Dino extinction
- 18 Dinosaurs around you
- 20 End of chapter: puzzles & activities
- 24 War-ready dinosaurs
- 26 Armored dinosaurs
- 32 End of chapter: puzzles & activities
- 36 Horn-faced dinosaurs
- 38 Ceratopsian dinosaurs
- 44 End of chapter: puzzles & activities
- 48 Plant-eating dinosaurs
- 50 Ornithopod dinosaurs
- 56 End of chapter: puzzles & activities
- 60 Long-necked dinosaurs
- 62 Sauropod dinosaurs
- 68 End of chapter: puzzles & activities
- 72 Meat-eating dinosaurs
- 74 Theropod dinosaurs
- 86 Record-breaking dinosaurs
- 88 End of chapter: puzzles & activities
- 96 Fun facts about dinosaurs

18

24

36

48

60

72

74

INTERACTIVE EXPERIENCE

 Scan the QR code with your device's camera or download a free QR code reader app. Many iPhone and Android devices include these features

 When you see the "Scan with your phone or tablet" prompt, use your device to scan the QR code, which looks like this

 Hold your mobile device over the image and watch it come to life! Your device needs to be connected to the internet for this to function

WHAT ARE DINOSAURS?

The word "dinosaur" means "terrible lizard," but dinosaurs are not lizards! Dinosaurs evolved from ancient reptiles, and while some looked a bit lizard-like, they were actually a really varied bunch. Some were small, speedy scavengers; some were huge, heavy plant-eaters and some were terrifying predators. There were dinosaurs with scales, feathers, crests, or spikes. Some dinosaurs had powerful jaws, sharp claws, wings, or even neck frills! Some dinosaurs walked on two legs and some walked on four. So if dinosaurs aren't lizards, and if they don't all look the same, then what makes a dinosaur a dinosaur?

All dinosaurs had these things in common, which helps scientists figure out if the skeleton they've discovered is a dinosaur or not:
- Their legs are directly under their bodies. Think about how lizards or crocodiles have legs that scheckmark out from the sides of their bodies and you can understand the difference.
- All dinosaurs are vertebrates, which means they have a backbone.
- All dinosaurs had some sort of tail.
- Dinosaurs were covered in scales or feathers.
- Dinosaurs laid eggs.

Dinosaurs first appeared in the Triassic period, about 235 million years ago. They continued to evolve through the Jurassic and Cretaceous periods. Some species of dinosaurs developed to be so powerful and ferocious that dinosaurs ruled the Earth. The Cretaceous period ended 66 million years ago when an enormous asteroid – a giant rock from space – hit Earth and wiped out almost all of the dinosaurs. All that is left of them now are their fossils, which include bones, teeth, and eggs. Dinosaurs existed for a very long time, so there are loads of fossils still waiting to be found. Scientists are learning more and more about these amazing creatures every day, and new species are still being discovered. Strangely enough, birds are the descendants of dinosaurs, so you could say that dinosaurs aren't actually extinct!

ODD ONE OUT

Which of these is **not** a dinosaur? Use the clues about what makes a dinosaur a dinosaur

A. T-REX
B. ARCHAEOPTERYX
C. CROCODILE
D. SNAKE
E. STEGOSAURUS

ANSWERS: C and D

WHAT ARE DINOSAURS?

FILL IN THE BLANKS

See if you can fill in these sentences using the word pool

1. Dinosaurs first appeared about _____ million years ago.

2. They were wiped out by an _____ that hit Earth _____ million years ago.

3. This means they existed on Earth for around _____ million years.

`235` `ASTEROID` `171` `66`

ANSWERS: 1. 235 2. Asteroid, 66 3. 171

WATCH THIS!
101 FACTS ABOUT DINOSAURS
SCAN WITH YOUR PHONE OR TABLET
https://bit.ly/3ulPgkS

WORD SCRAMBLE

Unscramble the words to spell out some dinosaur features

1. WSLAC
2. ALIT
3. KESSPI
4. ASERHEFT
5. EACSLS
6. HETEHT

ANSWERS: Claws, tail, spikes, feathers, scales, teeth

5

KINDS OF DINOSAURS

Dinosaurs can be grouped by their various features. This helps scientists and experts identify what kind of dinosaur they're talking about. Grouping dinosaurs in this way is called "classifying" them, and it can be really complicated and scientific. Here we are going to group the dinosaurs into five main categories: ornithopods, armored dinosaurs, ceratopsians, sauropods, and theropods.

Ornithopods are medium-sized plant-eaters that walked on two legs. When we say medium-sized, remember we are talking about dinosaurs, so medium-sized is about as big as an elephant! Ornithopods are known for having large nostrils. Most lived in herds and some developed colorful head-crests that they used for display. Ornithopods include Iguanodon, Edmontosaurus, Hadrosaurus, and Parasaurolophus.

Armored dinosaurs are dinosaurs that were covered in protective armor-like plating. These medium-sized plant-eaters walked on four legs and were protected by thick skin that was often covered in bony plates or spikes. Their tails often had spikes or a bony club at the end. They were slow movers – all that armor is heavy – but their armor helped protect them from predators. Armored dinosaurs include Ankylosaurus, Scelidosaurus, and Stegosaurus.

Ceratopsians are mostly known as four-legged plant-eaters with huge skulls topped with a bony frill and sometimes horns. But some ceratopsians walked on two legs and had no horns. A good way to identify a ceratopsian is to look at its mouth. It's actually a beak – it looks a lot like a parrot's! Ceratopsians include Triceratops, Protoceratops, and Liaoceratops.

Sauropods are the big ones – the long-necked, long-tailed, four-legged, leaf-eating dinosaurs. They could be as tall as a six-story building and as long as two-and-a-half buses. These dinosaurs had long necks to reach the uppermost branches on trees. Their teeth were broad and blunt for grinding up leaves. While they didn't have armored skin, their size and powerful tails were often enough to stop smaller carnivores from attacking them. Sauropods include Diplodocus, Apatosaurus, Argentinosaurus ,and Plateosaurus.

Theropods walked on two legs. They were mostly hunters, although some were plant-eaters. This was the most diverse of the dinosaur groups, with theropods ranging from small, feathered creatures to large, fierce predators. Modern-day birds evolved from theropods. Theropods include Tyrannosaurus rex, Herrerasaurus, Velociraptor, Allosaurus, Spinosaurus, and Archaeopteryx – a small, feathery one!

WORD WHEEL

How many dinosaur-related words can you make from the word wheel?

HOW MANY CAN YOU SPOT?

Look closely at the picture. How many sauropods can you see?

ANSWER: Six.

KINDS OF DINOSAURS

TYRANNOSAURUS
TIE-ran-oh-SAW-russ
THEROPOD KING OF THE DINOSAURS
HOW YOU PRONOUNCE MY NAME

FAVORITE FOOD
Smaller dinosaurs

WHERE I LIVED
Canada and US

HOW BIG I AM
Forty feet long

A FUN FACT ABOUT ME
Each of my sharp, curved teeth are about as big as a banana

ANKYLOSAURUS
an-KIE-loh-SAW-russ
ARMORED WALKING TANK
HOW YOU PRONOUNCE MY NAME

FAVORITE FOOD
Plants

WHERE I LIVED
North America

HOW BIG I AM
Twenty-three feet long

A FUN FACT ABOUT ME
The bony plates that cover my body are called osteoderms

SPINOSAURUS
SPY-noh-SAW-russ
THEROPOD FISH FORAGER
HOW YOU PRONOUNCE MY NAME

FAVORITE FOOD
Fish

WHERE I LIVED
Egypt and Morocco

HOW BIG I AM
Fifty feet long

A FUN FACT ABOUT ME
Scientists still have no idea what my back sail was used for

WHAT KIND OF DINOSAUR AM I?
Use the clues to identify the dinosaur group:

A
- Walks on four legs
- Has a long neck
- Eats leaves

B
- Two or four legs
- Has a bony frill on its head

C
- Walks on two legs
- Has very sharp teeth
- Eats meat

D
- Eats plants
- Skin is covered in bony plates

E
- Walks on four legs
- Has large nostrils

ANSWERS: A. Sauropod B. Ceratopsian C. Theropod D. armored dinosaur E. Ornithopod

STEGOSAURUS
STEG-o-SAW-russ
ARMORED, PROTECTED PLANT-EATER
HOW YOU PRONOUNCE MY NAME

FAVORITE FOOD
Low-lying plants

WHERE I LIVED
Europe and North America

HOW BIG I AM
Thirty feet long

A FUN FACT ABOUT ME
Some scientists call my spiky tail a thagomizer

TRICERATOPS
try-SERRA-tops
CERATOPSIANS THREE-HORNED HERBIVORE
HOW YOU PRONOUNCE MY NAME

FAVORITE FOOD
Low-lying plants

WHERE I LIVED
North America

HOW BIG I AM
Thirty feet long

A FUN FACT ABOUT ME
I weigh as much as about four rhinos

IGUANODON
ig-WAH-no-don
EUORNITHOPOD SOCIAL ANIMAL
HOW YOU PRONOUNCE MY NAME

FAVORITE FOOD
Plants and low branches

WHERE I LIVED
Europe

HOW BIG I AM
Forty feet long

A FUN FACT ABOUT ME
I love being sociable, so I live in a herd

DIPLODOCUS
dip-LOD-o-kuss
SAUROPOD GIANT PLANT-EATER
HOW YOU PRONOUNCE MY NAME

FAVORITE FOOD
Leaves right at the top of the tallest tree

WHERE I LIVED
North America

HOW BIG I AM
Eighty-five feet long

A FUN FACT ABOUT ME
I am as big as a blue whale

THE TRIASSIC PERIOD: 252-201 MILLION YEARS AGO

Life on Earth has existed for billions of years, but not all ancient creatures lived at the same time. Even among the dinosaurs, different species lived at different times. Ancient history is split into chunks of time called eras, and these are further split into smaller chunks of time called periods. The dinosaurs lived during the Mesozoic era, which is split into three periods: Triassic, Jurassic, and Cretaceous. Let's go back 252 million years, to the start of the Triassic period. Earth had just suffered its worst mass extinction event, known as the Permian Extinction. Most of the living creatures had been wiped out following terrible changes in temperature and gas concentrations in the atmosphere. But slowly, life started to bloom again. Lizards and ancient crocodile-like creatures stalked across the land. Huge marine reptiles swam through the ocean depths. Flying reptiles called pterosaurs dominated the skies. It was hot and dry, with most of the land covered in desert. Towards the end of the Triassic period, a new type of creature emerged on land. . . the first of the dinosaurs.

Eodromaeus is one of the earliest known dinosaurs. It was a small and light theropod, which meant it was fast and nimble – perfect for chasing small reptiles. Eodromaeus was only about as big as a guitar at a three feet long, and it weighed the same as a cat. Herrerasaurus was a bigger beast at around twenty feet in length. It was also a theropod, and was able to compete with the ancient crocodiles for food thanks to its sharp teeth, flexible jaw, and balanced body – but it probably wouldn't win in a fight against them! Some plant-eating dinosaurs existed in this time as well, including Plateosaurus, one of the earliest sauropods. Plateosaurus was a bit taller than a giraffe at around thirty-two feet long and had a long neck for reaching treetop leaves.

WHICH DINOSAURS LIVED DURING THIS PERIOD?

EODROMAEUS

HERRERASAURUS

PLATEOSAURUS

WHAT WAS IT LIKE DURING THE TRIASSIC PERIOD?

HOT, COLD, OR JUST RIGHT?
Hot and dry

AVERAGE TEMPERATURE	AVERAGE RAINFALL
62°F	Variable

SUMMARY
- Most of the land was covered in desert
- The deserts were too hot, so most animals lived in cooler, wetter coastal regions
- The supercontinent Pangaea was slowly drifting apart, forming smaller continents and climate zones
- Large reptiles hunted on land, while pterosaurs flew through the air and huge marine reptiles dominated the deep
- Small, agile dinosaurs appeared. They had to compete with or escape from the larger land reptiles

THE TRIASSIC PERIOD: 252-201 MILLION YEARS AGO

MATCH THE DINOSAUR TO THE ITEM MOST SIMILAR IN SIZE

ANSWERS: Eodromaeus - guitar, Herrerasaurus - door, Plateosaurus - giraffe

TRUE OR FALSE?

The Triassic period was the second period in the Mesozoic era
TRUE OR FALSE

There was only one continent on Earth at the start of the Triassic period
TRUE OR FALSE

Pterosaurs are a kind of dinosaur
TRUE OR FALSE

All of the early dinosaurs were carnivores
TRUE OR FALSE

The Triassic period was much hotter than it is on Earth today
TRUE OR FALSE

ANSWERS: False, true, false, false, true

WORD SEARCH

Can you find these words?

TRIASSIC HERRERASAURUS PANGAEA
PTEROSAUR PLATEOSAURUS MESOZOIC

THE JURASSIC PERIOD: 201-145 MILLION YEARS AGO

During the Jurassic period, the huge supercontinent of Pangaea split into two parts: Laurasia in the north and Gondwana in the south. A great ocean swept between the two continents, completely changing the Earth's climate. There were rainforests, lakes, and even tropical islands. Now that much more of the land was close to water, plants and animal life flourished. This was good news for the dinosaurs, who evolved into hundreds of diverse species depending on where they were in the world. Dinosaurs became the dominant land animal. Huge, plant-eating sauropods towered over the forests, ruthless theropod predators hunted across the plains and small, feather-covered dinosaurs chased their prey among the trees. During this time, the first birds and small mammals also appeared on Earth.

The Jurassic period saw dinosaurs that were larger and more powerful than ever before, including Allosaurus, Apatosaurus, Diplodocus, Stegosaurus, and Scelidosaurus. Allosaurus was one of the deadliest dinosaurs of all time. Not only did it have sharp teeth and claws for attacking its prey, it was also fast, intelligent, and fearless. Apatosaurus and Diplodocus were two long-necked plant-eaters. They had enormous tails that helped balance their bodies and could also pack a painful punch against any predator who tried to come close. Stegosaurus is famous for its tough body armor, the line of plates along its back and its spiky tail. These features helped protect the plant-eater from predators. Scelidosaurus was covered from head to tail with tough, bony plates. Even though this relatively small plant-eater was slow, its body armor was enough to keep attackers at bay. It's because of these mighty beasts that we can say without a doubt that during the Jurassic period, dinosaurs ruled Earth!

WHICH DINOSAURS LIVED DURING THIS PERIOD?

ALLOSAURUS

STEGOSAURUS

DIPLODOCUS

THE JURASSIC PERIOD: 201–145 MILLION YEARS AGO

IDENTIFY THE DINOSAURS

Draw a line between the dinosaur name and its silhouette

HERBIVORE OR CARNIVORE?

Were these dinosaurs herbivores (plant-eaters) or carnivores (meat-eaters)? Mark the boxes with H or C

ALLOSAURUS

APATOSAURUS

DIPLODOCUS

STEGOSAURUS

SCELIDOSAURUS

ANSWERS: C, H, H, H, H

SCELIDOSAURUS SKIN

Can you tell which of these shows the bony plates of a Scelidosaurus?

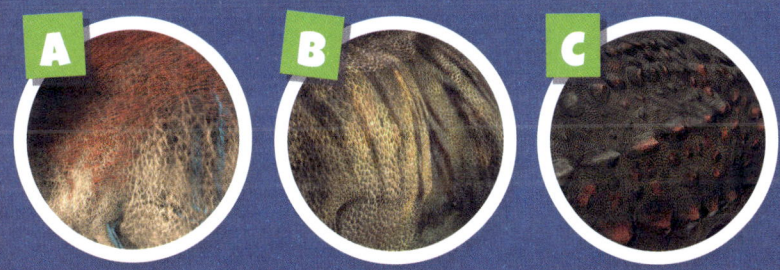

A B C

ANSWER: C

WHAT WAS IT LIKE DURING THE JURASSIC PERIOD?

HOT, COLD, OR JUST RIGHT?
Warm and humid

AVERAGE TEMPERATURE	AVERAGE RAINFALL
61°F	At least 45in

SUMMARY

- Dinosaurs were everywhere, in all shapes and sizes
- Different climate zones allowed diverse species to flourish
- Small insects, birds, and mammals lived among the dinosaurs.
- Enormous marine reptiles dominated the lakes and oceans
- Dinosaur battles were an everyday sight: ferocious predators attacked armored plant-eaters

SCELIDOSAURUS

APATOSAURUS

THE CRETACEOUS PERIOD: 145-66 MILLION YEARS AGO

QUIZ

CAN YOU ANSWER THESE QUESTIONS?

WHICH TWO CONTINENTS SPLIT INTO SMALLER CONTINENTS DURING THE CRETACEOUS PERIOD?
A. Britain and America
B. Laurasia and Gondwana
C. Europe and Asia

CAN YOU NAME A DINOSAUR THAT LIVED IN HERDS?
A. Cowasaurus
B. Tyrannosaurus
C. Iguanodon

WHAT TYPE OF PLANTS FIRST APPEARED IN THE CRETACEOUS PERIOD?
A. Deadly plants
B. Blue plants
C. Flowering plants

WHICH FLYING CREATURE WAS AS BIG AS A SMALL PLANE?
A. Quetzalcoatlus
B. Velociraptor
C. Triceratops

WHICH DINOSAUR HAD A CLUB AT THE END OF ITS TAIL?
A. Spinosaurus
B. Ankylosaurus
C. Iguanodon

ANSWERS: B, C, C, A, B

As the Jurassic period gave way to the Cretaceous period, dinosaurs still ruled the Earth. In fact, the Cretaceous period is when some of the most famous dinosaurs of all time lived: mighty Triceratops, deadly Velociraptor, and the ultimate predator, the Tyrannosaurus rex. While dinosaurs stomped, hunted, and roared, the Earth was changing.

The continents continued to shift and drift. Laurasia and Gondwana split into smaller continents, bringing the shape and layout of the continents closer to how the Earth looks today. Sea levels rose, which flooded many places, giving flying creatures a chance to develop. All of these changes created new environments and habitats, where a growing variety of plants, insects, and animals lived and evolved. Flowering plants appeared for the first time and attracted bees and other insects. Rodent-like mammals scurried across the ground on most continents. Birds became a more common sight among the pterosaurs who filled the skies. But it was the huge flying creatures, such as the Quetzalcoatlus – the size of a small airplane – that really thrived during these times.

Yet none of these new species were any match for the dinosaurs, who continued to dominate the animal world. Speedy Velociraptors chased their prey, ready to slash at them with razor-sharp claws. Fierce Tyrannosauruses battled against armored plant-eaters, such as Ankylosaurus, who fought back with powerful tail clubs. Clashes took place between Triceratops males to see who would lead the herd. Meanwhile, long-necked sauropods grazed in groups, swishing their enormous tails if predators dared to come near. Sail-backed Spinosaurus hunted for fish in lakes and rivers, while herds of elephant-sized Iguanodon searched for the best trees to munch on. Who knows if any creature would ever have evolved into something powerful enough to take on the dinosaurs? Perhaps they'd still be around today ruling the Earth, if it wasn't for the asteroid that crashed into our planet 66 million years ago, ending the Cretaceous period and wiping out the dinosaurs.

WHICH DINOSAURS LIVED DURING THIS PERIOD?

TRICERATOPS

TYRANNOSAURUS

THE CRETACEOUS PERIOD: 145–66 MILLION YEARS AGO

ODD ONE OUT

Which of these dinosaurs is the odd one out?

A
TYRANNOSAURUS

B
STEGOSAURUS

C
VELOCIRAPTOR

D
TRICERATOPS

E
IGUANODON

F
ANKYLOSAURUS

ANSWER: B

WHAT WAS IT LIKE DURING THE CRETACEOUS PERIOD?

HOT, COLD, OR JUST RIGHT?
Hot and humid

AVERAGE TEMPERATURE	AVERAGE RAINFALL
64°F	At least eight feet/year

SUMMARY
- As the continents became smaller and drifted apart, they each developed their own climate
- Different species evolved in new environments and habitats
- Dinosaurs were the dominant land animal, with a mix of carnivores and herbivores
- Flowering plants supported new species of insects, including bees
- The polar ice caps formed

VELOCIRAPTOR

ANKYLOSAURUS

SPINOSAURUS

IGUANODON

WHERE ARE THEY NOW?

Dinosaur remains have been found on every continent on Earth – even Antarctica. This is because the dinosaurs lived back when the continents were still drifting and changing. It all began as one huge continent, Pangaea, which split into two, becoming Laurasia and Gondwana. These continued to drift apart, eventually forming the seven continents we know today: North America, South America, Europe, Africa, Asia, Australasia, and Antarctica. This helps us understand why some species of dinosaur have been found in two different locations on Earth. It's possible that a certain type of dinosaur evolved in one place, but as the continents drifted apart, some dinosaurs went one way, while some went the other way. Maybe that's why Brachiosaurus fossils have been found in Africa and Europe, as well as in North America.

It's interesting to note that the most dinosaur fossils have been discovered in the hot deserts of North America, China, and Argentina. Desert climates prevent a lot of plant growth, and that helps protect underground fossils. In North America, dinosaur skeletons are still being discovered today. There's a layer of rock beneath the ground that runs across western North America. It's called the Morrison Formation, and it's an amazing source of dinosaur fossils. Allosaurus, Diplodocus, Stegosaurus, and Apatosaurus are just some of the dinosaurs that have been found here.

In China, there has been a recent surge in the number of dinosaur fossils discovered. The Yixian Formation in Liaoning, near Beijing, is famous for its perfectly preserved fossils – some of them show dinosaur feathers in incredible detail. These finds are helping scientists understand the links between dinosaurs and birds. In Argentina, the Anacleto Formation is a site full of fossils. Scientists discovered hundreds of dinosaur eggs here, which are actually really rare. Hopefully these discoveries will teach us something new about dinosaurs! Dinosaur fossils are everywhere. Perhaps most are discovered by professionals on fossil expeditions, but plenty have been found by amateurs, dinosaur lovers, and even regular people just going for a walk. Next time you visit an old forest, quarry, desert, or mountain, keep your eyes open. . . you might discover a fossil!

1 BRACHIOSAURUS
TYPE Sauropod
LOCATION Algeria
Brachiosaurus lived in Algeria, but also in Portugal, Tanzania, and the US

2 CRYOLOPHOSAURUS
TYPE Theropod
LOCATION Antarctica
Cryolophosaurus was the first dinosaur to be discovered in Antarctica

3 ARGENTINOSAURUS
TYPE Sauropod
LOCATION Argentina
Argentinosaurus was possibly the largest dinosaur ever

4 MUTTABURRASAURUS
TYPE Ornithopod
LOCATION Australia
An almost-complete skeleton of Muttaburrasaurus was found in Australia in 1963

5 STRUTHIOSAURUS
TYPE Armored
LOCATION Austria
Experts believe Struthiosaurus was probably a very small armored dinosaur that lived on islands

6 IGUANODON
TYPE Ornithopod
LOCATION Belgium
The first Iguanodon skeleton ever discovered was found by a British scientist in Sussex, England, in 1822

7 STAURIKOSAURUS
TYPE Theropod
LOCATION Brazil
The first Staurikosaurus skeleton was discovered at the Santa Maria Formation in Brazil in 1936

8 ALBERTOSAURUS
TYPE Theropod
LOCATION Canada
Albertosaurus is named after Alberta, the Canadian province where it was first discovered

9 ANTARCTOSAURUS
TYPE Sauropod
LOCATION Chile
The name doesn't refer to Antarctica, but to the Southern Hemisphere in general

10 MICRORAPTOR
TYPE Theropod
LOCATION China
Microraptor inhabited Asia. Its fossils have been found all over modern-day China.

11 SPINOSAURUS
TYPE Theropod
LOCATION Egypt
Spinosaurus fossils were first discovered in Egypt in 1912

12 MEGALOSAURUS
TYPE Theropod
LOCATION England
In 1824, Megalosaurus was the first dinosaur to be named

13 COMPSOGNATHUS
TYPE Theropod
LOCATION France
An almost-complete Compsognathus skeleton was found in France in 1971

14 ARCHAEOPTERYX
TYPE Theropod
LOCATION Germany
Scientists were astonished to find Archaeopteryx fossils with perfectly preserved outlines of the dinosaur's feathers

15 INDOSUCHUS
TYPE Theropod
LOCATION India
Three incomplete Indosuchus skulls were discovered in India

16 FUKUISAURUS
TYPE Ornithopod
LOCATION Japan
Fukuisaurus fossils were first discovered in 1989 in the Fukui Prefecture of Japan

17 JAXARTOSAURUS
TYPE Ornithopod
LOCATION Kazakhstan
Jaxartosaurus is named after the Jaxartes river that flows through Kazakhstan. The Jaxartes river is now known as the Syr Darya

18 HETERODONTOSAURUS
TYPE Ornithopod
LOCATION Lesotho
The first Heterodontosaurus skull was discovered in Lesotho in 1962

19 MAJUNGASAURUS
TYPE Theropod
LOCATION Madagascar
The first Majungasaurus fossils were discovered in Madagascar in 1896. They consisted of two teeth, a claw, and a few backbones

20 MALAWISAURUS
TYPE Sauropod
LOCATION Malawi
Malawisaurus fossils were first found in the Dinosaur Beds of Malawi – a rock formation where many dinosaur fossils have been found

21 VELOCIRAPTOR
TYPE Theropod
LOCATION Mongolia
Many fossils and fairly complete skeletons of Velociraptor have been discovered in Mongolia's Gobi Desert

22 DELTADROMEUS
TYPE Theropod
LOCATION Morocco
No skull fossils have ever been discovered, so scientists cannot be sure what Deltadromeus actually looked like

23 AFROVENATOR
TYPE Theropod
LOCATION Niger
Only one set of Afrovenator remains have ever been found. This is known as a holotype

24 ALLOSAURUS
TYPE Theropod
LOCATION Portugal
Allosaurus lived in the US as well as Portugal

25 ZALMOXES
TYPE Ornithopod
LOCATION Romania
Zalmoxes fossils were first discovered in 1899 in Transylvania

PSITTACOSAURUS
26 | TYPE Ceratopsian | LOCATION Russia

Up to twelve species of Psittacosaurus have been discovered across Asia

PLATEOSAURUS
30 | TYPE Sauropod | LOCATION Switzerland

Plateosaurus lived across western Europe more than 200 million years ago

TYRANNOSAURUS
34 | TYPE Theropod | LOCATION US

The first Tyrannosaurus remains discovered were teeth, found in Colorado in 1874

SALTOPUS
27 | TYPE Theropod | LOCATION Scotland

Just one set of Saltopus remains exist. This holotype was discovered in Scotland in 1910

GIRAFFATITAN
31 | TYPE Sauropod | LOCATION Tanzania

In 1906, a mining engineer in Tanzania spotted a huge Giraffatitan bone scheckmarking out of the ground

ARCHAEORNITHOMIMUS
35 | TYPE Theropod | LOCATION Uzbekistan

The first Archaeornithomimus fossils were found in Mongolia. More were found in Uzbekistan around thirty years later

COELOPHYSIS
28 | TYPE Theropod | LOCATION South Africa

Coelophysis was first discovered in the US, but more fossils were found in South Africa years later

NIGERSAURUS
32 | TYPE Sauropod | LOCATION Tunisia

Nigersaurus was originally discovered in Niger, but similar remains were later found in Tunisia

PANTYDRACO
36 | TYPE Ornithopod | LOCATION Wales

Pantydraco is named after the Pant-y-Ffynnon Quarry in Wales where it was discovered

ARAGOSAURUS
29 | TYPE Sauropod | LOCATION Spain

Aragosaurus remains were first discovered in the Villar del Arzobispo Formation in eastern Spain

LAPLATASAURUS
33 | TYPE Sauropod | LOCATION Uruguay

Laplatasaurus fossils were first discovered in Argentina

VULCANODON
37 | TYPE Sauropod | LOCATION Zimbabwe

When it was discovered, Vulcanodon was considered the earliest-known sauropod

WHERE ARE THEY NOW?

TRY THIS!

It must be exciting to discover dinosaur fossils. Here's a fun way you can do it at home

Find some of your favorite dinosaur models. Freeze one in a container filled with water. Wait a day until it's completely frozen and then remove it from the freezer. Allow it to sit for about ten minutes until you can remove the container. Place the ice block on a plate or tray and use a fork to carefully chip away at the ice until you discover your dinosaur "fossil."

WHERE IN THE WORLD?

Can you place these fantastic fossil spots on the map below?

A. **MORRISON FORMATION**
B. **YIXIAN FORMATION**
C. **ANACLETO FORMATION**

DID YOU KNOW?

When the Morrison Formation was first discovered to be such a great place to find dinosaur bones, two scientists began a heated rivalry to collect the most fossils – it was known as the Bone Wars.

DINO EXTINCTION

The dinosaurs evolved into the mightiest species of all time. They ruled the Earth thanks to their immense size and their powerful bodies. But there came a day when something much bigger and even more powerful arrived on Earth: an asteroid. This asteroid was a rock the size of Mount Everest, and it was hurtling through space at a speed of twelve miles per second. It struck Earth with enormous force, killing every living thing within the impact zone instantly.

The force of the impact caused huge tidal waves to surge out even further, destroying everything in their way. The impact of the asteroid also triggered volcanoes and earthquakes even further away, throwing lava, dust, and toxic gas into the air. Acid rain poured down into the seas and oceans, killing any marine animals near the surface.

Wildfires started across the planet, and they raged fiercely thanks to the gas in the air. The Earth became unimaginably hot. Any land animals who couldn't escape underground or deep under water died from the heat, fires, or toxic gases within a few hours of the impact. But it wasn't over yet. The dust and soot from the impact, volcanoes, and fires filled the air, blocking out the Sun completely. This is known as an "impact winter."

Without sunlight, the temperatures dropped and plants died across the whole planet. Plant-eaters were unable to find food, so they began to die out. Meat-eaters soon followed, as they had no prey to hunt. Every non-bird species of dinosaur became extinct, as did more than three-quarters of Earth's species. The survivors included birds, small mammals, sharks, lizards, and turtles – but even these species would have been reduced to just a few creatures who managed to find a safe place and enough food to survive until the dust cloud was gone and the Earth began to grow again.

1 AN ENORMOUS ASTEROID STRIKES EARTH
An asteroid ten miles wide hit the Earth, right where the country Mexico is today.

2 HUGE TIDAL WAVES DEVASTATE THE LAND
Waves 1,000 feet high surged from the point of impact, destroying everything in their paths.

3 WILDFIRES SPREAD
Wildfires spread across the land, destroying whole environments and the animals that lived there.

4 DUST CLOUDS FILL THE AIR
Dust from the asteroid impact, volcanic eruptions, and wildfires blocked out the Sun for a whole year.

5 EARTH COOLS DOWN AND BECOMES ALMOST UNINHABITABLE
Sunlight couldn't get through, so plants died. Creatures who were still alive couldn't find food.

6 MASS EXTINCTION
Most land creatures became extinct. Only those who managed to hide and live on very little survived.

DINO EXTINCTION

WORD SCRAMBLE

Can you unscramble these words?

1. IDETOSRA
2. ERISWIDFL
3. TONENCTXII

ANSWERS: 1. Asteroid 2. Wildfires 3. Extinction

TRUE OR FALSE?

AN IMPACT WINTER IS WHEN SNOW HITS THE GROUND VERY HARD

TRUE OR FALSE

ALL DINOSAURS WERE WIPED OUT BY THE ASTEROID

TRUE OR FALSE

THE ASTEROID STRUCK MEXICO

TRUE OR FALSE

ANSWERS: False, false, true

WHO SURVIVED?

EXTINCT
- EVERY NON-BIRD DINOSAUR, INCLUDING TYRANNOSAURUS AND TRICERATOPS WHO WERE ALIVE AT THE TIME
- MOST LAND ANIMALS
- MARINE REPTILES
- PTEROSAURS

SURVIVED
- BIRDS
- SHARKS
- FROGS
- SNAKES
- LIZARDS
- MAMMALS
- TURTLES
- SPIDERS

DISORDER

Can you rearrange these pictures into the order they took place?

A FREEZING CONDITIONS

B DEAD DINOSAURS

C ASTEROID COLLISION

D TIDAL WAVE

ANSWERS: C, D, A, B

DINOSAURS AROUND YOU

So that was the end of the dinosaurs. . . or was it? You'll be happy to know that dinosaurs are still around today. In fact, you are very familiar with them – you call them birds! Scientists agree that modern birds evolved from theropod dinosaurs. Think about it: three toes, sharp beaks, hollow bones, feathers, and they walk on two legs. Archaeopteryx was a theropod from the Jurassic period and is one of the earliest known birdlike dinosaurs. Archaeopteryx is a fascinating creature because it has both dinosaur features, like sharp teeth, a bony tail, clawed hands, and birdlike features such as wings, long feathers, and the ability to fly short distances. Archaeopteryx fossils have helped scientists understand the link between dinosaurs and birds.

Another helpful fossil is from a Cretaceous-period dinosaur called Confuciusornis. This crow-sized dinosaur lived millions of years after Archaeopteryx. It had evolved more birdlike features, including a toothless beak, long tail feathers, and three clawed fingers on the ends of its wings. As dinosaurs took to the skies, their wings became more important than their clawed hands. A sharp beak became more important than teeth. A feathered tail helped steer better than a bony tail. Look closely next time you see a bird. You will notice how similar it looks to a theropod dinosaur. There are some differences, of course, but it's pretty exciting to think that next time you look out of your window, you might see a living, breathing dinosaur.

If you're looking to get up close and personal with the dinosaurs of old, there are plenty of ways to do it. Dinosaur track sites have been discovered around the world, where you can walk in the footsteps of the dinosaurs. Ancient dinosaur footprints have been discovered in places like Scotland, Spain, the US, Canada, and Bolivia. The Morrison Formation in the US has loads of sites where you can see dinosaur footprints and fossils. You can even volunteer to join a dig for a day and find your own. And don't forget your local natural history museum. It will have its own collection of incredible dinosaur artifacts and fossils to be explored.

PICKET WIRE CANYONLANDS
COLORADO, US
The longest dinosaur tracks in North America include theropod and sauropod footprints.

QUARRY EXHIBIT HALL, DINOSAUR NATIONAL MONUMENT
UTAH, US
See real dinosaur fossils that are still in place where they were first discovered.

PARQUE CRETÁCICO, CAL ORCK'O
SUCRE, BOLIVIA
A cliff face covered with more than 5,000 footprints from at least eight species of dinosaur.

AN CORRAN BEACH
ISLE OF SKYE, SCOTLAND, UK
Walk alongside big dinosaur footprints on an ancient beach.

DINOSAURS AROUND YOU

STOMPING ABOUT

Different dinosaurs had different feet. For example, sauropod feet were round and broad to stop the great beasts from sinking into the ground. Can you draw a line between each dinosaur and its footprint?

A THEROPOD

B SAUROPOD

C CERATOPSIAN

D ORNITHOPOD

E ARMORED DINOSAUR

1

2

3

4

5

ANSWERS: A5, B1, C4, D2, E3

WINGING IT

As birds evolved, their wings became their most important feature. Flight gave birds their advantage, so they evolved to fly as smoothly as possible. Experiment with wing shapes on some paper airplane to see what shapes, sizes, or positions make your paper airplane fly best.

NOT SO DIFFERENT

Circle the birdlike features on this Archaeopteryx:

Circle the dinosaur-like features on this chicken:

END OF CHAPTER: PUZZLES & ACTIVITIES

LET'S PUT YOUR KNOWLEDGE TO THE TEST AND SEE HOW WELL YOU KNOW THE HISTORY OF THE DINOSAURS

HOW BIG?

Can you plot the heights of these dinosaurs on the graph to compare their size to an average human child?

VELOCIRAPTOR 1.5 FT
COELOPHYSIS 4 FT
TYRANNOSAURUS 18 FT
TRICERATOPS 9.8 FT
APATOSAURUS 29.5 FT
STEGOSAURUS 13 FT
ARGENTINOSAURUS 42 FT

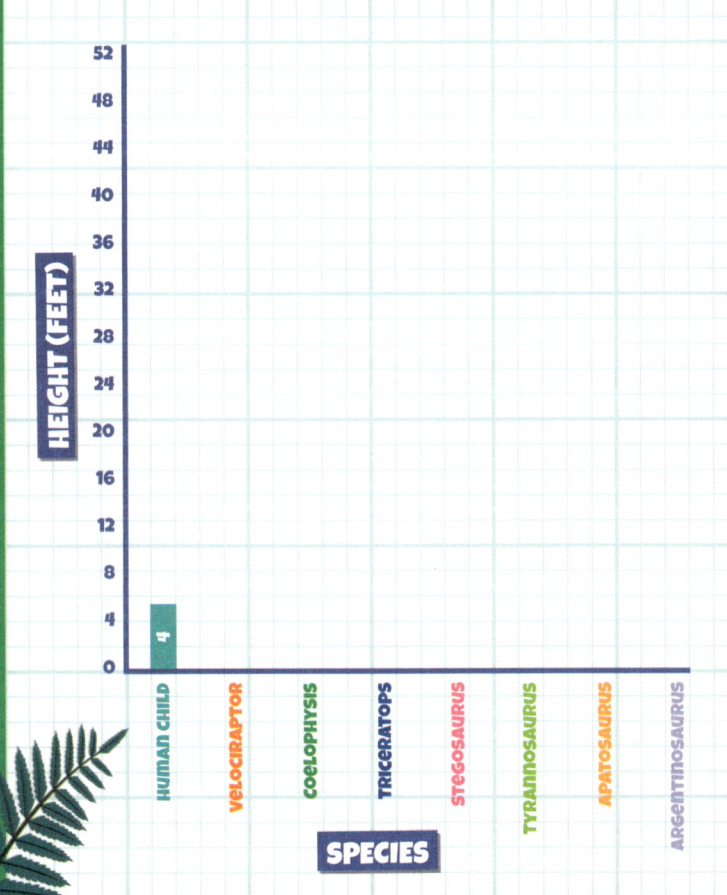

END OF CHAPTER: PUZZLES & ACTIVITIES

CROSSWORD

Using the clues below, can you work out which words fit in the blanks to fill out the crossword?

ACROSS
1. A rock from space that wiped out the dinosaurs (8)
3. What plant-eaters are called (10)
4. Sauropods had blunt _____ for grinding up leaves (5)
6. A plant-eater with a bony head frill and three horns (11)
9. Stegosaurus had these on its tail (6)
10. Dinosaurs laid _____ (4)
11. The Triassic, Jurassic, and Cretaceous periods make up the Mesozoic _____ (3)
13. When the asteroid hit Earth, a huge _____ cloud blocked out the Sun (4)

DOWN
2. The flying reptiles who lived at the same time as dinosaurs and are often mistaken for them (10)
4. Dinosaurs that walked on two legs and ate meat (9)
5. The time period in which the dinosaurs died out (10)
7. Some dinosaurs were covered in _____, although they couldn't fly (8)
8. Modern-day descendants of the dinosaurs (5)
12. The supercontinent that stretched across Earth when dinosaurs first appeared (7)

IDENTITY PARADE

Can you name the dinosaur from its silhouette?

A. B. C. D. E. F.

ANSWERS: 1. (Across) Asteroid 2. (Down) Pterosaurs 3. Herbivores 4. (Across) Teeth (Down) Theropods 5. Cretaceous 6. Triceratops 7. Feathers 8. Birds 9. Spikes 10. Eggs 11. Era 12. Pangaea 13. Dust

ANSWERS: A. Spinosaurus B. Stegosaurus C. Triceratops D. Diplodocus E. Apatosaurus F. Allosaurus

QUIZ

CAN YOU ANSWER THESE QUESTIONS ABOUT THE WORLD OF THE DINOSAURS?

HOW MANY YEARS AGO DID THE DINOSAURS FIRST APPEAR?
A. 5 years ago
B. 235 million years ago
C. 3.8 billion years ago

WHICH GROUP OF HUGE DINOSAURS HAD LONG NECKS TO EAT FROM THE TREETOPS?
A: Sauropods
B: Triceropods
C: Longneckopods

TYRANNOSAURS REX, ALLOSAURUS, AND VELOCIRAPTOR ARE ALL MEMBERS OF WHICH GROUP OF DINOSAURS?
A: Iguanopods
B: Theropods
C: Tyrannopods

WHAT WAS DINOSAUR SKIN COVERED IN?
A: Clothes and fabrics
B: Paint
C: Scales, plates, or feathers

WHAT IS A DINOSAUR FOSSIL?
A: The remains of a dinosaur, including bones, teeth, and eggs
B: Bone that is hidden in a tomb
C: A shell on the beach

ANSWERS: B, A, B, C, A

DESIGN YOUR OWN DINO

Look at the different dinosaur features below and draw a dinosaur of your own

Will your dinosaur be big, medium, or small?
Will your dinosaur walk on two legs or four?
Will your dinosaur have a long or short neck?
Will your dinosaur be covered in scales, plates, or feathers?
Will your dinosaur have a long, short, or dangerously spiky tail?
Will your dinosaur have horns, head frills, spikes, back plates, back sails, or anything else?
Will your dinosaur have sharp claws?
Will your dinosaur have sharp or blunt teeth?

SPOT THE DIFFERENCE

Can you spot six differences between these two pictures?

END OF CHAPTER: PUZZLES & ACTIVITIES

WHICH PICTURE SHOWS A DINOSAUR?

A: PTEROSAUR
B: SCELIDOSAURUS
C: CROCODILE

ANSWER: B

THINK ABOUT IT

We learned that almost all of the dinosaurs – along with seventy-five percent of Earth's species – were wiped out after the huge asteroid hit Earth. But twenty-five percent of Earth's species managed to survive. Discuss with your friends about how you think these survivors managed to stay alive after such a catastrophic event.

BUILD A 3D DINOSAUR MODEL

Dinosaurs were enormous, and scientists often marvel that they were able to support their own weight. Think about how heavy a Diplodocus neck must have been. Experts think some dinosaurs had hollow bones, which meant their bodies weren't too heavy to lift. Now it's time for you to think about how to make a dinosaur balance and hold its own weight. Let's build a 3D dinosaur model that can stand up on its own

WHAT YOU'LL NEED
- Paper
- Cardboard or paper plates
- Scissors
- Tape
- Markers

INSTRUCTIONS

1. Plan your dinosaur models on plain paper so you can be sure they are the right shape and size before you cut them out.
2. Use the paper templates to cut out the different parts of your dinosaur from cardboard or paper plates.
3. Decorate the different parts of your dinosaur. Will you create a realistic-looking dinosaur or a more unique creature?
4. Fit the parts together and use tape where necessary to build your model. Does it stand on its own? You might need to make small adjustments until you get the balance just right!

WORD SEARCH

Can you find these dinosaurs in the word search:

```
T Y R A N N O S A U R U S Y P A
A P T O L N Y A L J Y I E D O N
H I G U A N O D O N I T H O N K
E R D I P J L N P A U R U B S Y
R D I P L O D O C U S I L M P L
R L S O L U I G Y R A C O T I O
E N T L G K P L O S U E P Y N S
R P A S T E G O S A U R U S O A
A M R H Y H E L L J G A P T S U
S L U G R A U P S N M T L I A R
A P A T O S A U R U S O T A U U
U N U D L I U E T O U P I T R S
R O R S P L R O U T P S T H U O
U M L A H E M P A P R E A N S L
S A V E L O C I R A P T O R T H
```

- TYRANNOSAURUS
- STEGOSAURUS
- TRICERATOPS
- ANKYLOSAURUS
- IGUANODON
- HERRERASAURUS
- DIPLODOCUS
- APATOSAURUS
- VELOCIRAPTOR
- SPINOSAURUS

WAR-READY DINOSAURS

Armored dinosaurs are pretty easy to identify. Is the dinosaur's body covered in armor? Yes? Then it's an armored dinosaur. With their armor and solid build, the armored dinosaurs were about the same size and weight as a modern-day tank. They walked the Earth from the early Jurassic period until the end of the Cretaceous period, when they died out along with the rest of the dinosaurs. And when they walked the Earth, they walked it slowly, thanks to all that heavy armor.

Armored dinosaurs were herbivores, so they didn't need speed to chase or catch their food. And as for predators, the armored dinosaurs were very well protected. Not only did they have armor covering most of their body, many of them – including Ankylosaurus – had a bony club at the end of their tails. Others, including Stegosaurus, had spikes on their tails. This made their tails powerful weapons that could easily injure an attacking Allosaurus.

Their armor was made up of bony plates and bumps called osteoderms. It was extremely tough, seeing as it was made out of bone. As if all that wasn't enough, most armored dinosaurs had spikes or spines somewhere on their bodies – another way to keep predators away. Stegosaurus is famous for the plates and spikes that stand in a line down its back and tail, but other armored dinosaurs also boasted face horns, shoulder spikes, and tail spines.

These walking tanks had small brains but big stomachs, so they were able to eat huge amounts of plants and grass. Famous armored dinosaurs include Ankylosaurus, Stegosaurus, Kentrosaurus, Scelidosaurus, Hesperosaurus, and Minmi.

WHAT MAKES AN ARMORED DINOSAUR?

- ✓ Medium-sized
- ✓ Walked on four legs
- ✓ Plant-eater
- ✓ Body covered in bony armor called osteoderms
- ✓ Defensive features including body armor, horns, spikes, spines, and tail clubs

MISSING WORDS

Complete the sentences

1. Armored dinosaurs lived from the early _____ period to the end of the Cretaceous period.
2. Armored dinosaurs had _____ brains and _____ stomachs.
3. The bony plates and bumps on the armored dinosaurs were called _____.
4. The _____ of armored dinosaurs often had a club or spikes at the end.

OSTEODERMS   SMALL   TAILS   JURASSIC   BIG

ANSWERS: 1. Jurassic 2. Small, big 3. osteoderms 4. tails

WATCH THIS!
THE WORLD'S BEST PRESERVED ARMORED DINOSAUR

SCAN WITH YOUR PHONE OR TABLET

https://bit.ly/38Ltuip

ODD ONE OUT

Which of these dinosaurs is not an armored dinosaur?

A — MINMI

B — ANKYLOSAURUS

C — STEGOSAURUS

D — KENTROSAURUS

E — ALLOSAURUS

F — HESPEROSAURUS

ANSWER: E

ARMORED DINOSAURS

There are two main types of armored dinosaurs: ankylosaurs and stegosaurs. I'm sure you can guess which groups Ankylosaurus and Stegosaurus belong to! Ankylosaur armor is made up of rows of small, bony bumps. Most ankylosaurs have horns on their faces and a club at the end of their tails. Stegosaurs are different – they have longer necks; their armor is made up of bony plates; they usually have rows of upright plates, spikes, or spines along their backs and they generally have spikes on their tails, not clubs. Most of the stegosaurs died out before the Cretaceous period, so you would never have seen a Stegosaurus doing battle with a Tyrannosaurus!

ANKYLOSAURUS
an-KIE-loh-SAW-russ *(HOW YOU PRONOUNCE MY NAME)*

MY FAVORITE FOOD — Plants
HOW MUCH I WEIGH — Four tons
HOW BIG I AM — Twenty-three feet in length
HOW BIG I AM COMPARED TO YOU
I am about as tall as an adult, but much longer
REGION I LIVED IN
I lived in North America, across where both Canada and the US are today
ABOUT ME
I'm one of the most famous armored dinosaurs. I love roaming the land, munching on plants, and long grass. My tough body armor is enough to convince most predators to stay away. And if any come close, one whack from my club tail will drive them off.

MATCH UP

Match the features to the correct group of armored dinosaurs

- SMALL BONY BUMPS
- LARGE PLATES ALONG BACK
- SPIKY TAIL
- TAIL CLUB
- FACE HORNS
- LONGER NECK

ANKYLOSAURS

STEGOSAURS

CHUNGKINGOSAURUS
chung-king-oh-SAW-russ *(HOW YOU PRONOUNCE MY NAME)*

MY FAVORITE FOOD — Plants
HOW MUCH I WEIGH — One-and-a-half tons
HOW BIG I AM — Thirteen feet in length
HOW BIG I AM COMPARED TO YOU
I'm about the same size as a car
REGION I LIVED IN — China
ABOUT ME
I am one of the smaller stegosaurs, but don't let that fool you. I have two rows of sharp spikes along my back and some very strong spikes on my tail. My teeth are flat to help me grind up the plants I eat.

WATCH THIS!
LISTEN TO THIS SONG ABOUT ANKYLOSAURUS
SCAN WITH YOUR PHONE OR TABLET
https://bit.ly/3LRce9y

EDMONTONIA
ed-MON-toh-KNEE-yah *(HOW YOU PRONOUNCE MY NAME)*

- **MY FAVORITE FOOD** — Plants
- **HOW MUCH I WEIGH** — Three tons
- **HOW BIG I AM** — Thirteen feet in length
- **HOW BIG I AM COMPARED TO YOU** — I'm a bit bigger than a large rhino
- **REGION I LIVED IN** — Canada
- **ABOUT ME** — As one of the earlier ankylosaurs, my tail doesn't have a club at the end. Sometimes I wish it did, but I can still defend myself against predators thanks to my very thick armor made up of closely packed osteoderms and my four larger shoulder spikes.

EUOPLOCEPHALUS
you-OH-plo-KEFF-ah-luss *(HOW YOU PRONOUNCE MY NAME)*

- **MY FAVORITE FOOD** — Plants
- **HOW MUCH I WEIGH** — Two tons
- **HOW BIG I AM** — Twenty-three feet in length
- **HOW BIG I AM COMPARED TO YOU** — I am about as big as a minivan
- **REGION I LIVED IN** — Canada and the US
- **ABOUT ME** — I'm not afraid of meat-eaters. I might be slow, but my tail can swing at very high speeds. The bony club at the end is strong enough to break a dinosaur's leg! I also have spikes on my back and head – even my eyelids are armored.

DACENTRURUS
dah-SEN-troo-russ *(HOW YOU PRONOUNCE MY NAME)*

- **MY FAVORITE FOOD** — Plants
- **HOW MUCH I WEIGH** — Four tons
- **HOW BIG I AM** — Twenty feet in length
- **HOW BIG I AM COMPARED TO YOU** — I'm about as tall as an adult, but as long as an elephant
- **REGION I LIVED IN** — I lived in Europe in what is now England, France, and Portugal
- **ABOUT ME** — I was the first stegosaur to be discovered. I have two rows of plates along my back, and they become more like spikes as they continue down my tail. My name means "pointed tail," a feature I am very proud of.

GARGOYLEOSAURUS
GAR-goy-LEEH-oh-SAW-russ *(HOW YOU PRONOUNCE MY NAME)*

- **MY FAVORITE FOOD** — Plants
- **HOW MUCH I WEIGH** — 1,873 pounds
- **HOW BIG I AM** — Thirteen feet in length
- **HOW BIG I AM COMPARED TO YOU** — I'm about as big as a dolphin, but much heavier
- **REGION I LIVED IN** — The US
- **ABOUT ME** — I'm quite small for an ankylosaur, but that's alright. My sideways-facing plates keep predators away. I'm quite unusual because my plates are hollow at the base. This means I'm not as heavy as some other ankylosaurs.

GASTONIA
Gas-TOE-nee-ah *(HOW YOU PRONOUNCE MY NAME)*

- **MY FAVORITE FOOD** Plants
- **HOW MUCH I WEIGH** Two tons
- **HOW BIG I AM** Fifteen feet in length
- **HOW BIG I AM COMPARED TO YOU** I'm around the same size as an adult hippo
- **REGION I LIVED IN** The US
- **ABOUT ME** I don't have a tail club but I do have plenty of spikes all along my tail – and all over the rest of my body too. I am most proud of my two backwards-facing shoulder spikes. They are a great defense against even the fiercest predators.

KENTROSAURUS
ken-TROH-saw-russ *(HOW YOU PRONOUNCE MY NAME)*

- **MY FAVORITE FOOD** Plants
- **HOW MUCH I WEIGH** One ton
- **HOW BIG I AM** Sixteen feet in length
- **HOW BIG I AM COMPARED TO YOU** I'm as big as a tractor
- **REGION I LIVED IN** Tanzania in modern-day Africa
- **ABOUT ME** I have quite a long neck for an armored dinosaur, so I can reach some leaves that other stegosaurs cannot. My brain is about the size of a walnut, but I have a great sense of smell. Best of all, I have amazing long spikes.

HESPEROSAURUS
hess-per-oh-SAW-russ *(HOW YOU PRONOUNCE MY NAME)*

- **MY FAVORITE FOOD** Plants
- **HOW MUCH I WEIGH** Three tons
- **HOW BIG I AM** Twenty feet in length
- **HOW BIG I AM COMPARED TO YOU** I'm about three times as tall as an adult human
- **REGION I LIVED IN** The US
- **ABOUT ME** I have two rows of back plates and four tail spikes. I look pretty similar to my much more famous cousin, Stegosaurus – although my back plates are a bit longer!

HUAYANGOSAURUS
hoy-ANG-oh-SAW-russ *(HOW YOU PRONOUNCE MY NAME)*

- **MY FAVORITE FOOD** Plants
- **HOW MUCH I WEIGH** One ton
- **HOW BIG I AM** Fifteen feet in length
- **HOW BIG I AM COMPARED TO YOU** I'm about the size of a great white shark
- **REGION I LIVED IN** China
- **ABOUT ME** I am a relative of Stegosaurus, but I'm about half the size – and I lived about 10 million years earlier. The plates along my back are taller and spikier than those of many other stegosaurs, but my tail spikes are quite similar to the rest of my kind.

WATCH THIS! ANIMATRONIC HUAYANGOSAURUS
SCAN WITH YOUR PHONE OR TABLET
https://bit.ly/38I86dK

ARMORED DINOSAURS

MINMI
min-mie *(HOW YOU PRONOUNCE MY NAME)*

MY FAVORITE FOOD Plants and seeds
HOW MUCH I WEIGH 661 pounds
HOW BIG I AM Ten feet in length
HOW BIG I AM COMPARED TO YOU About three times as tall as an adult human
REGION I LIVED IN Australia

ABOUT ME
I was the first ankylosaur found in the Southern Hemisphere. I am lucky to have armor on my belly as well as my back, unlike most armored dinosaurs, and I am also proud to be a faster runner than my armored friends.

COLOR ME
What color will your Ankylosaurus be?

PINACOSAURUS
pin-AK-oh-saw-russ *(HOW YOU PRONOUNCE MY NAME)*

MY FAVORITE FOOD Plants
HOW MUCH I WEIGH One ton
HOW BIG I AM Sixteen-and-a-half feet in length
HOW BIG I AM COMPARED TO YOU I'm only as tall as a toddler, but I am much longer
REGION I LIVED IN China and Mongolia

ABOUT ME
I roam the Asian deserts in a herd, searching for plants or grass to eat. I am protected from predators, such as Velociraptors, by the bony plates and spikes along my back. The club on my tail is huge – it packs a powerful punch.

POLACANTHUS
pohl-ah-KAN-thuss *(HOW YOU PRONOUNCE MY NAME)*

MY FAVORITE FOOD Plants
HOW MUCH I WEIGH Two tons
HOW BIG I AM Sixteen feet in length
HOW BIG I AM COMPARED TO YOU I'm about as tall as a door
REGION I LIVED IN The UK

ABOUT ME
My name means "many spines," and I love that description. I do indeed have many spines along my back and tail. I also have one huge plate that covers my lower back and protects my hips from predators.

DID YOU KNOW?
The plates that protected the armored dinosaurs were covered in tough keratin – the same thing that your fingernails are made of!

SAUROPELTA
SORE-oh-pelt-ah *(HOW YOU PRONOUNCE MY NAME)*

MY FAVORITE FOOD Plants
HOW MUCH I WEIGH Two-and-a-half tons
HOW BIG I AM Twenty-one feet in length
HOW BIG I AM COMPARED TO YOU
I am longer than a giraffe is tall
REGION I LIVED IN The US
ABOUT ME
I am one of the larger armored dinosaurs. I don't have a tail club, but I'm known for my large shoulder and neck spines. They scheckmark out to the sides, which keeps predators far away from my head!

SCELIDOSAURUS
skell-EYE-doh-saw-russ *(HOW YOU PRONOUNCE MY NAME)*

MY FAVORITE FOOD Plants
HOW MUCH I WEIGH 705 lbs
HOW BIG I AM Thirteen feet long
HOW BIG I AM COMPARED TO YOU
I'm probably just a little taller than you
REGION I LIVED IN In the UK
ABOUT ME
I am one of the earliest armored dinosaurs, which is why I am quite small. I search for food near the rivers and swamps of Laurasia, trusting that my flat, spiky osteoderms will protect me from predators.

SCUTELLOSAURUS
SKOO-tell-oh-saw-russ *(HOW YOU PRONOUNCE MY NAME)*

MY FAVORITE FOOD Plants
HOW MUCH I WEIGH Twenty-two pounds
HOW BIG I AM Four feet in length
HOW BIG I AM COMPARED TO YOU
I'm probably about your size
REGION I LIVED IN The US
ABOUT ME
I am one of the only ankylosaurs that can run on two legs as well as four. Unlike most armored dinosaurs, I am quite light and speedy. My body has some armor for protection, but I can usually escape my predators by simply running away.

STEGOSAURUS
STEG-oh-SAW-russ *(HOW YOU PRONOUNCE MY NAME)*

MY FAVORITE FOOD Plants
HOW MUCH I WEIGH Four tons
HOW BIG I AM Thirty feet in length
HOW BIG I AM COMPARED TO YOU
I'm as big as a minibus
REGION I LIVED IN The US and Europe
ABOUT ME
I'm one of the giant armored dinosaurs, famous for the two rows of tough plates that run down my back and my four-spiked tail. Predators know better than to mess with me while I'm eating.

ARMORED DINOSAURS

WORD SEARCH

```
T O L M P A N K S R H J I L O P
U S A R L H L D L B P E O T A N
D T D H S N T E S A U R Q A R O
R E I L A U R G P E Q E D E M L
B O P U P L A T E S K F T R O P
A D R A G O N A L U P U R H R E
D E T H K L Y E J R O P E F R T
E R H K I D W L Y I P L G L O H
B M N L P E D P N L J A L I P F
N S K A N K Y L O S A U R U S A
J P L P O J L R M P R I L P Q S
M E N L S G M J C E M E P E U D
I R E I A B G A L A R D E R M F
L S R R U N R I U F A L A S K N
P L A N T S E P B H S M F L Z M
```

ANKYLOSAURUS **PLATES** **ARMOR**
OSTEODERMS **CLUB** **PLANTS**

TRY IT OUT

Can you list animals or objects that are similar in size to most of the armored dinosaurs?

TALARURUS
ta-la-ROO-russ

HOW YOU PRONOUNCE MY NAME

MY FAVORITE FOOD Plants

HOW MUCH I WEIGH One-and-a-half tons

HOW BIG I AM Twenty feet in length

HOW BIG I AM COMPARED TO YOU
I'm probably about your height, but as long as a crocodile

REGION I LIVED IN Mongolia

ABOUT ME
I'm one of the later ankylosaurs, living in the late Cretaceous period. My rectangular, beak-like mouth is the perfect shape for grazing on plants and long grasses. My body armor consists of bony bumps and a strong tail club.

END OF CHAPTER: PUZZLES & ACTIVITIES

GIVE SOME PUZZLES ABOUT THE MIGHTY ARMORED DINOSAURS A TRY

MODEL ARMOR

Armored dinosaurs evolved with many defensive features to keep them safe from fast, meat-eating predators – from armored plates and tail clubs to shoulder spikes and osteoderms in all shapes and sizes. Create your own model armored dinosaur with customized armor.

WHAT YOU'LL NEED
- Modeling clay, dough, salt dough, clay, preferably in at least two colors

INSTRUCTIONS
1. Choose your dinosaur shape and mold its body from the modeling clay.
2. Use modeling clay of a different color to form your armor. You can make lots of little osteoderms or big, sharp spikes.
3. Place your armor onto your dinosaur. Think carefully about how the armor will help keep your dinosaur safe.

STEGOSAURUS SKIN
WHAT DID DINOSAUR SKIN LOOK LIKE?

SCAN WITH YOUR PHONE OR TABLET
https://bit.ly/3JD1U49

ARMORED DINOSAURS BY NUMBERS

Read through the chapter and fill in the boxes with the missing numbers:

- [ ] ANKYLOSAURUS FACE HORNS
- [ ] KENTROSAURUS SHOULDER SPIKES
- [ ] EDMONTONIA SHOULDER SPIKES
- [ ] SAUROPELTA TAIL CLUBS
- [ ] POLACANTHUS LOWER-BACK PLATES
- [ ] GASTONIA BACKWARDS-FACING SHOULDER SPIKES

ANSWERS: 4, 2, 4, 0, 2, 1

WHO AM I?

Identify the dinosaurs by studying their stats

1
- **LENGTH** 15 feet
- **WEIGHT** 2 tons
- **TAIL** Spikes but no club
- **OTHER FEATURES** Two backwards-facing shoulder spikes

2
- **LENGTH** 19.6 feet
- **WEIGHT** 3.8 tons
- **TAIL** Pointed
- **OTHER FEATURES** Two rows of plates down my back

ANSWERS: 1. Gastonia 2. Dacentrurus

DESIGN YOUR OWN ARMORED DINOSAUR

Think about all the features the armored dinosaurs shared. Now design your own. Remember, it must be protected from predators. Will you use plates, bumps, spikes, spines, tails clubs, horns, or a combination?

FILL ME IN

Half of this Stegosaurus is missing. Can you draw the missing parts in?

QUIZ

LET'S SEE HOW MUCH YOU'VE LEARNED ABOUT ARMORED DINOSAURS

NAME THE TWO MAIN TYPES OF ARMORED DINOSAUR
A. Ankylosaur only
B. Stegosaur only
C. Ankylosaur and stegosaur

WHAT ARE OSTEODERMS MADE FROM?
A: Bone
B: Skin
C: Teeth

HOW MANY SPIKES DOES A STEGOSAURUS HAVE ON ITS TAIL?
A: Four
B: Two
C: Six

CAN YOU NAME THE ANKYLOSAUR THAT DOESN'T HAVE A TAIL CLUB?
A: Ankylosaurus
B: Pinacosaurus
C: Gastonia

WHAT DO ARMORED DINOSAURS EAT?
A: Meat
B: Plants
C: Chips

WHY DO ARMORED DINOSAURS MOVE SO SLOWLY?
A: Their legs don't have strong muscles
B: Their armor is heavy
C: They've got nowhere to be

WHERE DID MINMI LIVE?
A: Africa
B: South America
C: Australia

ANSWERS: C, A, A, B, B, C.

CROSSWORD

ACROSS
1. Where an ankylosaur has its club (4)
2. Long, thin osteoderms that scheckmark up away from the body (6)
3. What predators do to their prey (6)
4. A twenty-foot stegosaur who looks very similar to Stegosaurus (13)
7. The slow, relaxed way armored dinosaurs walked the Earth (4)
10. An ankylosaur from Canada that has no club on its tail (10)

DOWN
2. Long, sharp osteoderms that scheckmark up away from the body (6)
3. Hard bones, plates, and osteoderms made up the _____ of the armored dinosaurs (6)
4. Some dinosaurs, including Pinacosaurus, lived in groups called _____ (5)
5. The period when the first armored dinosaurs appeared (8)
6. The technical name for each of the bony plates, spikes, spines, and bumps that covered the armored dinosaurs' bodies (9)
8. An ankylosaur only found in Australia (5)
9. What osteoderms are made of (4)
11. Plants and grass are the _____ of the armored dinosaurs (4)

ANSWERS: (Across) 1. Tail 2. Spines 3. Attack 4. Hesperosaurus 7. Roam 10. Edmontonia (Down) 2. Spikes 3. Armor 4. Herds 5. Jurassic 6. Osteoderm 8. Mimmi 9. Bone 11. Food Secret answer: Polacanthus

GIVE IT A GO!

In the crossword, you might notice some of the letters are in yellow squares. Unscramble the letters and you'll get the name of a many-spined ankylosaur.

WORD SCRAMBLE

Can you uncover the scrambled words?

1. **NAAGSOIT**
2. **ORMRA**
3. **EETMOSDOR**
4. **AYLUKORSAUNS**
5. **LNPSTA**

ANSWERS: Gastonia, armor, osteoderm, ankylosaurus, plants

END OF CHAPTER: PUZZLES & ACTIVITIES

TRUE OR FALSE?

THE ARMORED DINOSAURS DIED OUT BEFORE THE CRETACEOUS PERIOD
TRUE ☐ OR FALSE ☐

STEGOSAURUS IS AS BIG AS A MINIBUS
TRUE ☐ OR FALSE ☐

AN ANKYLOSAURUS" TAIL CLUB COULD BREAK A PREDATOR'S LEG
TRUE ☐ OR FALSE ☐

ARMORED DINOSAURS COULD REACH THE TOPMOST LEAVES ON THE TREES
TRUE ☐ OR FALSE ☐

ARMORED DINOSAURS HAD VERY SMALL BRAINS
TRUE ☐ OR FALSE ☐

ANSWERS: False, true, true, false, true

THINK ABOUT IT

If the armored dinosaurs were so well-protected, how did their predators stand a chance? Discuss with your friends what you think about the armored dinosaurs, their protective armor and their possible weak spots.

CREATE A DINOSAUR SWAMP

Many armored dinosaurs, including Scelidosaurus, lived in the swamps of the Jurassic period. If you have model or toy dinosaurs, why not build them their own swamp habitat? This activity can get messy, so make sure you ask an adult to help you cover the floor before you get started. Or better yet, do it outside!

WHAT YOU'LL NEED
- Large plastic tray
- Blue or green jelly, or use clear jelly and add food coloring
- Grass, herbs, or cress
- Twigs
- Other outdoor finds, for example pine cones or pebbles
- Model dinosaurs

INSTRUCTIONS
1. Make the jelly according to the instructions on the packet. If you need to add food coloring, add just a few drops. Once mixed, leave this to cool in the fridge.
2. Once the jelly is ready, pour it into the tray. It should break up as you pour it in. Stir it until it's gooey and messy enough for your swamp. A mix of big and little chunks of jelly is good.
3. Add clumps of grass or even pots of cress or herbs to the corners of your swamp. You could empty the pots into the swamp for a muddier look.
4. Complete your swamp by placing twigs and other outdoor finds into your jelly swamp to give it the perfect look. Now your swamp is ready for its dinosaur inhabitants. Place your figures into their new home.

MEMORY GAME

Write down the names of all the armored dinosaurs you've read about. Read through them and try to remember them. Then turn the paper over and try to write them all out from memory.
How many can you remember?

HORN-FACED DINOSAURS

Ceratopsians lived in the Cretaceous period, although some may have appeared in the late Jurassic. The word "ceratops" means "horned face" – and yes, most ceratopsians do have horns on their faces or heads. but not all of them! What ceratopsians all had in common was that they were herbivorous and had parrot-like beaks. They used these pointed beaks to select the most nutritious foods from the plants and vegetation of the prehistoric world. They also had amazing teeth to chop and grind their food very easily. Ceratopsians are perhaps most famous for their bony head or neck frills.

The most famous ceratopsian is probably Triceratops, who had three horns and a huge, impressive frill at the back of its head. Scientists think the frills were not much use as defensive weapons and that they were actually used for display: either to attract a mate or to show dominance within the herd. Whoever had the biggest, most colorful frills would fight to lead their herds.

While ceratopsians traveled long distances in search of food, they were not particularly fast. They had fairly thick skin, but their main defense against predators was their horns. Some of the largest ceratopsian horns ever discovered were around 4 feet long!

While Triceratops and other late ceratopsians walked on four legs, not all ceratopsians looked the same. Earlier ceratopsians, such as Psittacosaurus, were much smaller. They walked on two legs, had very small head frills and no horns. They still had the parrot-like beak, though. All of the ceratopsian dinosaurs were wiped out with most other dinosaurs of the Cretaceous period after the asteroid struck Earth.

ODD ONE OUT

Which of these dinosaurs is not an ceratopsian dinosaur?

A HORNS **B** HEAD FRILL **C** TAIL CLUB

ANSWER: C, D

HORN-FACED DINOSAURS

WHAT MAKES A CERATOPSIAN DINOSAUR?

- ✓ Parrot-like beak
- ✓ Bony head or neck frills
- ✓ Many have horns, but not all

WHAT DO YOU THINK?

Why do you think ceratopsians evolved from smaller, two-legged dinosaurs to larger, four-legged dinosaurs with big horns and head frills?

WATCH THIS!
A TOUGH DINOSAUR
SCAN WITH YOUR PHONE OR TABLET
https://bit.ly/3uyWqBb

D FANGS

E PARROT-LIKE BEAK

CERATOPSIAN DINOSAURS

Ceratopsians are a diverse group of dinosaurs. Some walked on two legs, some on four. Some had enormous neck frills and others had tiny frills. Some had huge, intimidating horns, while others had no horns at all! The only thing that really helps scientists identify a ceratopsian is the curved upper beak. There are three main groups of ceratopsians: psittacosaurids, protoceratopsids, and ceratopsids.

Psittacosaurids include the earliest, smallest ceratopsians, who had no horns and walked on two legs, such as Psittacosaurus and Yinlong. Protoceratopsids are the earliest four-legged ceratopsians, including Protoceratops and Leptoceratops, who could walk on two or four legs. The protoceratopsids were generally smaller than their later relatives. Finally, there are the ceratopsids, the largest ceratopsian dinosaurs with big frills and horns, such as Triceratops and Styracosaurus.

ALBERTACERATOPS
al-BERT-ah-serra-tops *(HOW YOU PRONOUNCE MY NAME)*

- **MY FAVORITE FOOD**: Plants
- **HOW MUCH I WEIGH**: Four tons
- **HOW BIG I AM**: Twenty-three feet in length
- **HOW BIG I AM COMPARED TO YOU**: I'm as big as a killer whale
- **REGION I LIVED IN**: Canada and the US
- **ABOUT ME**: I've been told I look unusual for a ceratopsian. I have two brow horns but no nose horn. Instead I have a curved ridge of bone on my nose and two curved hooks on my spiky neck frill.

COLOR ME
Color in this family of Triceratops

ARCHAEOCERATOPS
AR-kay-oh-serra-tops *(HOW YOU PRONOUNCE MY NAME)*

- **MY FAVORITE FOOD**: Low-lying plants
- **HOW MUCH I WEIGH**: Twenty-two pounds
- **HOW BIG I AM**: Four feet in length
- **HOW BIG I AM COMPARED TO YOU**: I'm about the size of a big dog
- **REGION I LIVED IN**: China
- **ABOUT ME**: I'm one of the earliest Cretaceous ceratopsians. My name means "ancient horned face," even though I have no horns. I do have a large skull though, and a long tail with long, thin spines along it. I walk on my two hind legs.

CERATOPSIAN DINOSAURS

FOSSIL FIND
MEET THE MOST COMPLETE TRICERATOPS FOSSIL EVER DISCOVERED

SCAN WITH YOUR PHONE OR TABLET
https://bit.ly/3IKjemO

DID YOU KNOW?
A giant bone bed was discovered in Canada containing hundreds of Centrosaurus fossils. Scientists think a herd drowned while crossing a river millions of years ago.

CENTROSAURUS
sen-tro-SAW-russ *(HOW YOU PRONOUNCE MY NAME)*

- **MY FAVORITE FOOD**: Tough plant material
- **HOW MUCH I WEIGH**: One ton
- **HOW BIG I AM**: Twenty feet in length
- **HOW BIG I AM COMPARED TO YOU**: I'm a little bigger than a rhinoceros
- **REGION I LIVED IN**: Canada
- **ABOUT ME**: I'm quite small compared to my larger cousin Triceratops, but I think my frill and spikes make up for it. My frill is quite big and there are two forwards-facing spikes at the top of it which make me quite unique.

CHAOYANGSAURUS
chow-yahng-SAW-russ *(HOW YOU PRONOUNCE MY NAME)*

- **MY FAVORITE FOOD**: Plants
- **HOW MUCH I WEIGH**: Twenty-two pounds
- **HOW BIG I AM**: Four feet in length
- **HOW BIG I AM COMPARED TO YOU**: I'm about the size of a raccoon
- **REGION I LIVED IN**: China
- **ABOUT ME**: I'm one of the earliest known ceratopsian dinosaurs. I had no horns, but if you look closely, you'll see I had a very slight frill and lovely little spikes all over my face and neck.

CERATOPSIAN SCRAMBLE
Unscramble the words to discover five ceratopsian dinosaurs

1. HRHCIRSANOSUAPUY
2. OMAUSCRAHSUS
3. UOISNIARSUE
4. TRAROTOEPPSCO
5. CAORTSSARUYUS

ANSWERS: 1. Pachyrhinosaurus. 2. Chasmosaurus. 3. Einiosaurus. 4. Protoceratops. 5. Styracosaurus.

CHASMOSAURUS
KAZ-moe-SAW-russ *(HOW YOU PRONOUNCE MY NAME)*

MY FAVORITE FOOD Plants
HOW MUCH I WEIGH Three tons
HOW BIG I AM Sixteen feet in length
HOW BIG I AM COMPARED TO YOU
I'm as big as a large crocodile
REGION I LIVED IN Canada
ABOUT ME
I have three horns on my face and rows of scales down my back. My neck frill is so big, it makes me seem taller than I am. You wouldn't know it, but the frill has holes in it which are covered over by skin.

COAHUILACERATOPS
koh-AH-hwee-la-SERRA-tops *(HOW YOU PRONOUNCE MY NAME)*

MY FAVORITE FOOD Plants
HOW MUCH I WEIGH Five tons
HOW BIG I AM Twenty-three feet long
HOW BIG I AM COMPARED TO YOU
I'm around the size of an elephant
REGION I LIVED IN Mexico
ABOUT ME
I'm a big beast with enormous horns on my brows. They are among the largest dinosaur horns ever. My head frill is narrower and taller than many other ceratopsians, and it has small spikes all around the edges. My back and tail are lined with a row of small spines.

EINIOSAURUS
EYE-nee-oh-SAW-russ *(HOW YOU PRONOUNCE MY NAME)*

MY FAVORITE FOOD Plants
HOW MUCH I WEIGH One-and-a-half tons
HOW BIG I AM Twenty feet in length
HOW BIG I AM COMPARED TO YOU
I'm about the size of a large family car
REGION I LIVED IN The US
ABOUT ME
You can't miss the two huge horns on top of my frill. I use these to scare predators away, and sometimes it works. I also have a big, downwards-pointing horn on my nose and small, bony ridges above my eyes.

KOSMOCERATOPS
KOZ-moe-SERRA-tops *(HOW YOU PRONOUNCE MY NAME)*

MY FAVORITE FOOD Plants
HOW MUCH I WEIGH One-and-a-half tons
HOW BIG I AM Fifteen feet in length
HOW BIG I AM COMPARED TO YOU
I'm about as big as a hippo
REGION I LIVED IN North America
ABOUT ME
My skull is huge, but that's not the most amazing thing about me. I have more horns than any other ceratopsian: fifteen. I have one nose horn, two brow horns, two cheek horns, and ten horns on my frill.

CERATOPSIAN DINOSAURS

DID YOU KNOW?
The skull of the Pentaceratops was the largest of any land animal ever. A skull measuring 8.7 feet long has been found – that's bigger than an adult human.

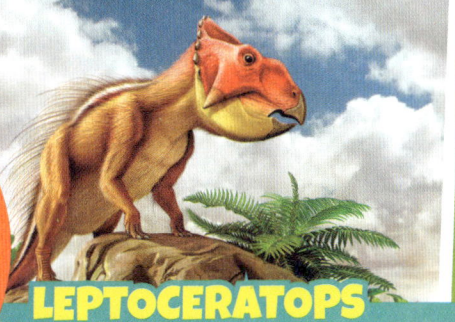

LEPTOCERATOPS
lep-toh-SERRA-tops *(HOW YOU PRONOUNCE MY NAME)*

- **MY FAVORITE FOOD**: Tough plant material
- **HOW MUCH I WEIGH**: 220 pounds
- **HOW BIG I AM**: Ten feet in length
- **HOW BIG I AM COMPARED TO YOU**: I'm as big as a tiger
- **REGION I LIVED IN**: Canada and the US
- **ABOUT ME**: I lived in the late Cretaceous period, when most ceratopsians were really big. However, I'm fairly small and can walk on my hind legs as well as on all fours. I don't have a huge neck frill and my cheek horns are very small, so I'm quite an unusual ceratopsian for my time.

PACHYRHINOSAURUS
pak-ee-rine-oh-SAW-russ *(HOW YOU PRONOUNCE MY NAME)*

- **MY FAVORITE FOOD**: Plants
- **HOW MUCH I WEIGH**: Three-and-a-half tons
- **HOW BIG I AM**: Twenty feet in length
- **HOW BIG I AM COMPARED TO YOU**: I'm about the size of a small elephant
- **REGION I LIVED IN**: Canada
- **ABOUT ME**: I'm tall for a ceratopsian, so I don't need a high frill. My frill extends back, not up, and has many horns growing on it and around the edges. I don't have a nose horn, but I have something called a nasal boss instead – a wide bulge perfect for headbutting my rivals.

PENTACERATOPS
PEN-ta-SERRA-tops *(HOW YOU PRONOUNCE MY NAME)*

- **MY FAVORITE FOOD**: Plants
- **HOW MUCH I WEIGH**: Seven tons
- **HOW BIG I AM**: Twenty-six feet in length
- **HOW BIG I AM COMPARED TO YOU**: My legs are taller than a human child
- **REGION I LIVED IN**: The US
- **ABOUT ME**: I'm one of the biggest ceratopsians. My skull is actually the largest skull around. I am fiercely proud of my beautiful, tall neck frill and the five horns on my face. If anyone dares to compete with me, I will battle them to prove my dominance.

PROTOCERATOPS
PRO-toe-SERRA-tops *(HOW YOU PRONOUNCE MY NAME)*

- **MY FAVORITE FOOD**: Desert plants
- **HOW MUCH I WEIGH**: 400 pounds
- **HOW BIG I AM**: Six feet in length
- **HOW BIG I AM COMPARED TO YOU**: I'm the size of a sheep
- **REGION I LIVED IN**: China and Mongolia
- **ABOUT ME**: I'm one of the earliest of the larger, four-legged ceratopsians, but I'm also one of the smallest. I have a small horn on my face and none on my neck frill, but my tough skin helps me survive in the desert, where I care for my young.

PSITTACOSAURUS
sit-ak-oh-SAW-russ
HOW YOU PRONOUNCE MY NAME

MY FAVORITE FOOD — Plants and seeds
HOW MUCH I WEIGH — 110 pounds
HOW BIG I AM — Six-and-a-half feet in length
HOW BIG I AM COMPARED TO YOU
I'm about as big as a sea lion
REGION I LIVED IN
China, Mongolia, and Russia
ABOUT ME
I'm one of the earliest and smallest ceratopsians. My body is covered in scales and there is a row of hollow bristles along my tail, similar to a porcupine's. I walk on two legs, but my young walk on four.

STYRACOSAURUS
sty-RAK-oh-SAW-russ
HOW YOU PRONOUNCE MY NAME

MY FAVORITE FOOD — Plants
HOW MUCH I WEIGH — Three tons
HOW BIG I AM — Eighteen feet in length
HOW BIG I AM COMPARED TO YOU
I'm as big as a great white shark
REGION I LIVED IN — Canada and the US
ABOUT ME
I'm extremely proud of my fancy frill. It has six spikes along the top, which I use to attract a mate. I also have a very sharp nose horn and a row of little spikes running all the way down from my frill to my tail.

TOROSAURUS
toh-row-SAW-russ
HOW YOU PRONOUNCE MY NAME

MY FAVORITE FOOD — Plants
HOW MUCH I WEIGH — Five tons
HOW BIG I AM — Twenty-four-and-a-half feet
HOW BIG I AM COMPARED TO YOU
My skull and frill are as big as a car
REGION I LIVED IN — Canada and the US
ABOUT ME
My frill is the largest of any ceratopsian. It also has five pairs of small hornlets along the back. I also have immense, sharp brow horns and a short nose horn, which help me scare away approaching predators.

TRICERATOPS
try-SERRA-tops
HOW YOU PRONOUNCE MY NAME

MY FAVORITE FOOD — Tough palm fronds
HOW MUCH I WEIGH — Nine tons
HOW BIG I AM — Thirty feet in length
HOW BIG I AM COMPARED TO YOU
I'm taller than a basketball hoop and as big as a whale shark
REGION I LIVED IN — The US
ABOUT ME
I am among the largest of the ceratopsians, and definitely the most famous. My name means "three-horned face" because I have three horns on my face. My two brow horns are as long as broom handles and my big, wide neck frill makes me seem even larger than I am.

CERATOPSIAN DINOSAURS

YINLONG
yin-long
HOW YOU PRONOUNCE MY NAME

- **MY FAVORITE FOOD** Plants
- **HOW MUCH I WEIGH** Thirty-three pounds
- **HOW BIG I AM** Four feet in length
- **HOW BIG I AM COMPARED TO YOU** I'm the size of a giant tortoise
- **REGION I LIVED IN** China
- **ABOUT ME** I'm one of the earliest ceratopsians. I walk on two legs. My long tail helps me balance. I only have a very tiny frill around my head and no horns.

DID YOU KNOW?
One of the most famous dinosaur finds showed a Protoceratops and Velociraptor mid battle. They were both killed by a collapsing sand dune.

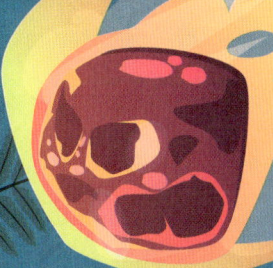

PUT ME IN MY PLACE
Draw a line to match these dinosaurs with their groups

- PSITTACOSAURIDS
- PROTOCERATOPSIDS
- CERATOPSIDS

- CHASMOSAURUS
- YINLONG
- LEPTOCERATOPS

ANSWERS: Chasmosaurus-Ceratopsids, Yinlong-Psittacosaurids, Leptoceratops-Protoceratopsids

ZUNICERATOPS
ZOO-nee-SERRA-tops
HOW YOU PRONOUNCE MY NAME

- **MY FAVORITE FOOD** Plants
- **HOW MUCH I WEIGH** 441 pounds
- **HOW BIG I AM** Ten feet in length
- **HOW BIG I AM COMPARED TO YOU** I'm the same size as a cow
- **REGION I LIVED IN** The US
- **ABOUT ME** I look similar to my cousin Triceratops, but I'm less than half its size. I also lived twenty-five million years earlier. I don't have a nose horn or horns on my frill, but I have long brow horns that grow even longer as I get older.

WHO AM I?
Identify the dinosaurs by studying the stats

1

- **LENGTH** Thirty feet
- **FACE HORNS** 3
- **FRILL** Big and wide

2

- **LENGTH** Six feet
- **FACE HORNS** 1
- **FRILL** Big and wide

3
- **LENGTH** Twenty-six feet
- **FACE HORNS** 5
- **FRILL** Tall

4

- **LENGTH** 24.6 feet
- **FACE HORNS** 3
- **FRILL** The biggest of all

ANSWERS: 1. Triceratops 2. Protoceratops 3. Pentaceratops 4. Torosaurus

END OF CHAPTER: PUZZLES & ACTIVITIES

WHAT HAVE YOU LEARNED ABOUT CERATOPSIAN DINOSAURS?

THINK ABOUT IT

A famous fossil find in Mongolia contained the well-preserved skeletons of a Protoceratops and Velociraptor who died mid-battle in the Gobi Desert. The Velociraptor's sharp claw lies deep in the Protoceratops" neck, but the Protoceratops has clamped its teeth around the Velociraptor's arm. Which dinosaur do you think would have won if the battle continued? Discuss with your friends.

WATCH THIS!
BRINGING A PSITTACOSAURUS TO LIFE FROM A FOSSIL

SCAN WITH YOUR PHONE OR TABLET

https://bit.ly/3LpmqpG

DESIGN YOUR OWN HEAD FRILL

Let's get creative and design a fancy frill for your favorite ceratopsian. To make it symmetrical, we're going to paint half the frill on the paper and then fold our paper over to make the other half an exact match

WHAT YOU'LL NEED
- Paper
- Pencil
- Paints

INSTRUCTIONS

1. Fold your paper in half down the middle so you know where the center of your frill will be.
2. Draw the outline of one half of your frill on one side of the paper. It can be any shape you like.
3. Paint your design onto half of the paper in a thick layer. Will you add a wavy frill? Spots of color? Horns? A nasal boss?
4. While your paint is still wet, fold the paper over and press it hard together. When you open it up, your symmetrical ceratopsian frill will be complete.

CERATOPSIANS BY NUMBERS

Read through the chapter and fill in the boxes with the missing numbers

- [ ] **EINIOSAURUS: DOWNWARD-POINTING NOSE HORNS**
- [ ] **CENTROSAURUS: FORWARD-FACING FRILL SPIKES**
- [ ] **KOSMOCERATOPS: HORNS**
- [ ] **PACHYRHINOSAURUS: NASAL BOSSES**
- [ ] **TOROSAURUS: PAIRS OF HORNLETS ALONG THE BACK OF ITS FRILL**

ANSWERS: 1, 2, 15, 1, 5

END OF CHAPTER: **PUZZLES & ACTIVITIES**

MAZE THROUGH THE DESERT

Can you help the Protoceratops find its way through the desert to its nest where its eggs are waiting?

PSITTACOSAURUS PUZZLE

Which piece fits to complete the picture of the Psittacosaurus?

QUIZ

HOW MANY QUESTIONS CAN YOU ANSWER?

WHAT DOES "CERATOPS" MEAN?
A. Horned face
B. Scarred face
C. Nosy dinosaur

CAN YOU NAME THE THREE MAIN CERATOPSIAN GROUPS?
A: Ceratopsids, psittacosaurus, tyrannosaurus
B: Kosmoceratops, frillosaurids, protoceratopsids
C: Psittacosaurids, protoceratopsids, ceratopsids

WHAT IS THE NAME OF THE BONE THAT GIVES CERATOPSIANS THEIR PARROT-LIKE BEAK?
A: Funny bone
B: Rostral
C: Incisor

WHAT DO CERATOPSIANS USE THEIR FRILLS FOR?
A: There is no reason
B: To attract a mate and show dominance
C: To make a sound

NAME ONE OF THE EARLIEST CERATOPSIANS
A: Yinlong
B: Psittacosaur
C: T-Rex

WHICH CERATOPSIAN COULD WALK ON TWO LEGS OR FOUR LEGS?
A: Einiosaurus
B: Torosaurus
C: Leptoceratops

WHICH CERATOPSIAN HAD THE MOST HORNS?
A: Psittacosaurus
B: Kosmoceratops
C: Pachyrhinosaurus

ANSWER: B

ANSWERS: A, C, B, B, A, C, B

WATCH THIS!
THE TOUGHEST OF ALL DINOSAURS: TRICERATOPS VS TYRANNOSAURUS REX

SCAN WITH YOUR PHONE OR TABLET

https://bit.ly/3uyWqBb

WHERE IN THE WORLD?

Ceratopsian fossils have been found in North America, Europe, and Asia. Can you color those continents in on the map below?

CROSSWORD

Below are some words you will have come across as you learned about ceratopsians. Can you fit them into the crossword?

- CHASMOSAURUS
- CERATOPSIAN
- PENTACERATOPS
- PLANTS
- SKULL
- FRILL
- SPIKE
- HORNS
- BEAK

END OF CHAPTER: PUZZLES & ACTIVITIES

MEMORY GAME

Write down the names of all the ceratopsians you've read about. Read through them and try to remember them. Then turn the paper over and try to write them all out from memory.
How many can you remember?

FILM A STOP MOTION DINOSAUR MOVIE

It's time to test your filmmaking skills! Grab your model dinosaurs and create a stop motion movie of your favorite ceratopsians in action. Will you film a battle scene between a Triceratops and a T-Rex or show a herd of Protoceratops roaming across the plains? Like the ceratopsians, creating stop motion isn't fast. You need patience. But the end result can be amazing. There are lots of stop motion apps available for free, or alternatively you can create your movie by taking photographs on your phone or camera and turning them into a slideshow.

WHAT YOU'LL NEED

- Phone or camera
- Tripod (optional)
- Model dinosaurs
- Lamp for lighting
- Props or background scenery
- Stop motion app or a computer to create a slideshow

INSTRUCTIONS

1. Find a suitable place for your movie and prepare the scene. Think about the background and what props you will need.
2. Make sure the lighting is good enough. Film outdoors or use a lamp to make sure your dinosaurs aren't in the dark.
3. If you have a tripod, set it up facing the scene. A tripod will help keep the camera still while you arrange the dinosaurs ready for the next shot. If you don't have a tripod, set your phone up somewhere it will be still and secure.
4. Take your first photo of the scene.
5. Make a small change to your scene so that the next photograph will show "movement."
6. Take another photo. Be careful not to move the camera between shots.
7. Repeat steps five and six until you have completed your scene. You should have lots of photos, each with just a small change from the last one.
8. Use an app or slideshow maker to run your photos one after the other. It should give the effect of a short movie, with your dinosaurs moving around.
9. Show your amazing stop motion movie to your friends and family. Start dreaming up the scene for your next movie.

A YINLONG SENTENCE

Using the letters of the word Yinlong, create a sentence. How funny or silly can you make it? Here's an example:

YOUR IGLOO NEVER LIES ON NUTRITIOUS GRASS

PLANT-EATING DINOSAURS

The plant-eating ornithopods were sort of like the cows of the dinosaur world: they lived in herds and were a common sight, grazing on the prehistoric plains and woodlands. In fact, ornithopods were the most common dinosaurs of all. Ornithopod means "bird feet," and most ornithopod dinosaurs were able to walk like birds – using two legs with birdlike, three-or-four-toed feet. And that's not the only feature they share with birds. Nearly all ornithopods have a beak, too, some with teeth and some without. In fact, ornithopods had the same ancestors as the other beaked dinosaurs, the ceratopsians.

The earliest ornithopods appeared in the Late Triassic period; they continued to thrive and evolve right until the end of the Cretaceous period, when they were wiped out with the rest of the dinosaurs. Early ornithopods, such as Heterodontosaurus, were small and speedy. They would dart on two legs through trees and shrubland, searching for food and hiding from predators.

Over millions of years, ornithopods grew larger and their bodies evolved to make it easier to eat plants and shrubs from the ground, with their backbones growing in a curved shape. With a curved back, ornithopods such as Iguanodon and Muttaburrasaurus found it easier to walk on four legs while grazing – though they could still run fast on their two stronger back legs if a hungry Allosaurus came roaring along. Other predators that hunted ornithopods included Deinonychus, Troodon, and the terrifying Tyrannosaur. The only defensive weapon an ornithopod had against a predator was a thumb spike on their front legs, though many later ornithopods don't seem to have this spike at all.

Early ornithopods had sharp teeth for slicing and tearing up leaves and plants, but later ornithopods developed very specialized teeth that allowed them to chew plant matter so that they didn't need to swallow it whole. These chewing teeth were called dental batteries, and they were actually made up of hundreds of teeth in a row that would grind together to mash up food.

Iguanodon – perhaps the most famous ornithopod – was one of the first dinosaurs to be discovered. In 1822, a British scientist named Mary Ann Mantell found some strange fossils on the side of a road. Her husband Gideon was a scientist too, and he identified them as the bones of a creature similar to an iguana, but much bigger.

WATCH THIS!
WHO WERE THE ORNITHOPODS

SCAN WITH YOUR PHONE OR TABLET
https://bit.ly/3LUqUoh

ORNITHOPOD OR NOT?

Spot which of these dinosaurs is an ornithopod. Put a checkmark in the correct boxes

IGUANODON

APATOSAURUS

MUTTABURRASAURUS

STEGOSAURUS

ALLOSAURUS

CORYTHOSAURUS

ANSWERS: Iguanodon, Muttaburrasaurus, Corythosaurus

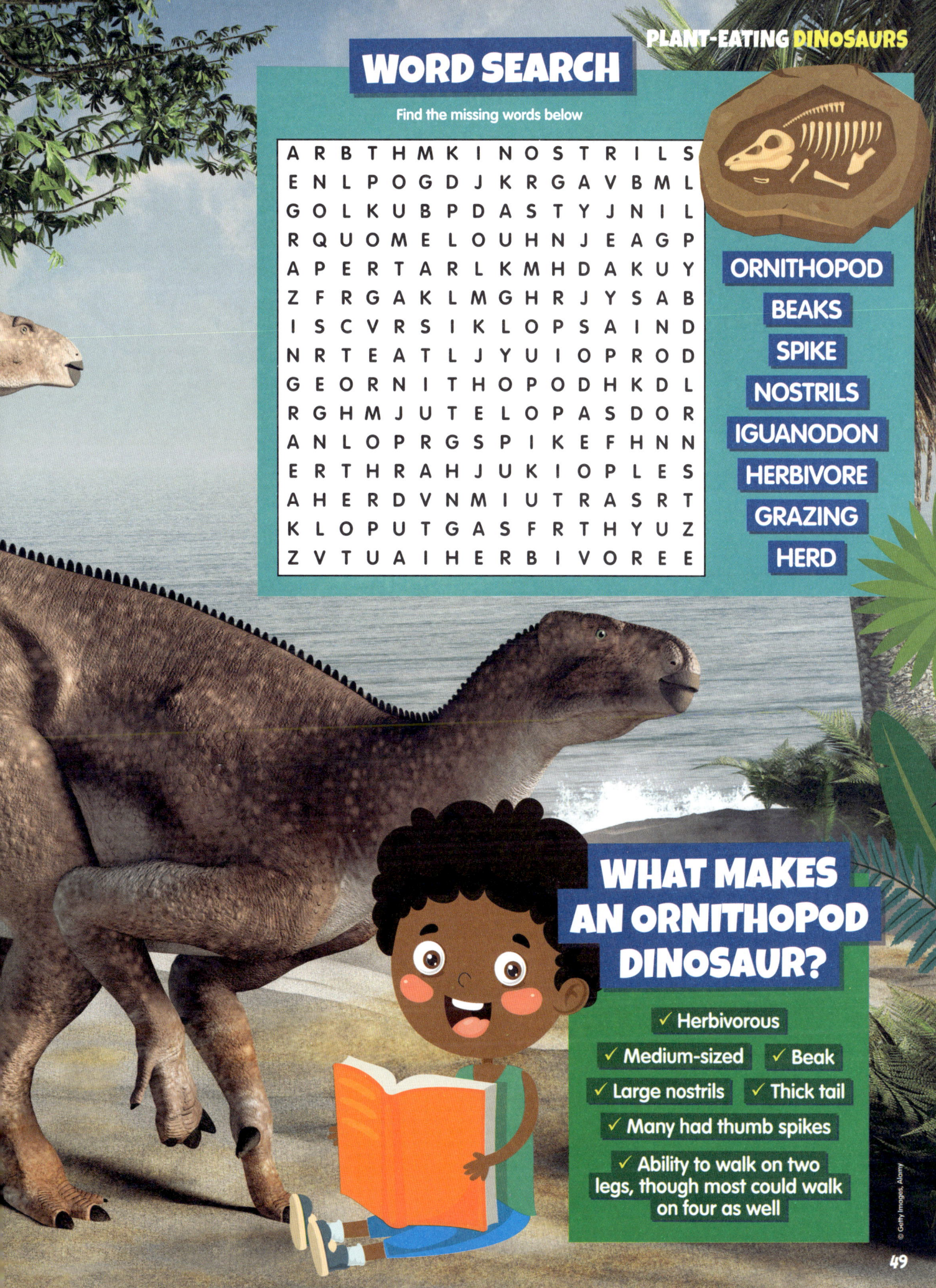

ORNITHOPOD DINOSAURS

Ornithopods are most famous for the evolution of their teeth, which eventually enabled them to fully chew their food before swallowing it. This helped make them the most successful dinosaurs of all time. By the early Cretaceous period, there were more ornithopods around than any other dinosaur group. As they evolved, ornithopods grew more specialized, which meant they were better equipped to feed and survive in their own environments. The most well-known group of ornithopods are the hadrosaurs, who are also known as the duckbill dinosaurs thanks to the shape of their beaks, which were flat, wide, and toothless, like duck bills. Hadrosaurus is the most typical example of a hadrosaur: strong back legs, smaller front legs, a large body, stiff tail, duckbill beak, a smaller or non-existent thumb spike, and dental batteries. Other hadrosaurs include Shantungosaurus and Parasaurolophus, who had a large head crest, another feature of many hadrosaurs. Hadrosaur head crests may have been used for display – to help the dinosaur attract a mate or show dominance – or to make their calls louder so they could communicate with their herd across longer distances. Speaking of herds, scientists have found clear evidence that ornithopods were social creatures. While they probably didn't go to many parties, they did live in herds, and they built nests close to each other and raised their young together.

ALTIRHINUS
al-te-RY-nuss *(HOW YOU PRONOUNCE MY NAME)*

- **MY FAVORITE FOOD** — Plants
- **HOW MUCH I WEIGH** — Two tons
- **HOW BIG I AM** — Twenty-three feet in length
- **HOW BIG I AM COMPARED TO YOU** — The size of a minibus
- **REGION I LIVED IN** — Asia
- **ABOUT ME** — Like many ornithopods, I have small front legs, but I can walk on all four. I have a useful gap between my beak and back teeth so I can tear off plants and chew at the same time. This helps me eat more efficiently.

COLOR THAT CREST

Parasaurolophus is famous for its crest, which was the largest of any ornithopod crest. Fossils show it was probably longer than three feet! Decorate this Parasaurolophus crest to show how amazing it might have looked in real life

CAMPTOSAURUS
CAMP-toe-SAW-russ *(HOW YOU PRONOUNCE MY NAME)*

- **MY FAVORITE FOOD** — Plants
- **HOW MUCH I WEIGH** — One ton
- **HOW BIG I AM** — Twenty-three feet in length
- **HOW BIG I AM COMPARED TO YOU** — I'm the size of an elephant
- **REGION I LIVED IN** — The UK and the US
- **ABOUT ME** — I walk on four legs when grazing, but when a predator comes close I run on my two back legs because they are stronger. I travel in a herd for safety and I'm happiest munching on plants and grinding them up with my many teeth.

ORNITHOPOD DINOSAURS

CORYTHOSAURUS
ko-RITH-oh-SAW-russ *(HOW YOU PRONOUNCE MY NAME)*

- **MY FAVORITE FOOD** — Plants
- **HOW MUCH I WEIGH** — Four tons
- **HOW BIG I AM** — Thirty feet in length
- **HOW BIG I AM COMPARED TO YOU** — As long as a bus
- **REGION I LIVED IN** — Canada and the US
- **ABOUT ME** — I can run pretty fast on my hind legs and I have hundreds of grinding teeth in my dental battery, but I'm most proud of my cool head crest. It looks a bit like a helmet and is filled with tubes which help me make a loud sound when I blow out through my nose.

DRYOSAURUS
DRY-o-SAW-russ *(HOW YOU PRONOUNCE MY NAME)*

- **MY FAVORITE FOOD** — Plants
- **HOW MUCH I WEIGH** — 220 pounds
- **HOW BIG I AM** — Ten feet in length
- **HOW BIG I AM COMPARED TO YOU** — About as big as a tiger
- **REGION I LIVED IN** — Tanzania and the US
- **ABOUT ME** — I store food in my cheeks, which is a very useful trick – especially when I'm roaming somewhere that doesn't have much to eat. When a predator such as Allosaurus tries to chase me, I run away quickly thanks to my strong leg muscles.

EDMONTOSAURUS
ed-MON-toe-SAW-russ *(HOW YOU PRONOUNCE MY NAME)*

- **MY FAVORITE FOOD** — Plants and leaves
- **HOW MUCH I WEIGH** — Six tons
- **HOW BIG I AM** — Forty feet in length
- **HOW BIG I AM COMPARED TO YOU** — I'm as big as a helicopter
- **REGION I LIVED IN** — Canada
- **ABOUT ME** — I might be big, but I'm fast. I can even outrun a T-Rex. I like to rear up on my back legs to eat tasty leaves from trees. My wide duckbill beak is good for tearing off leaves, and my cheek teeth grind them up for me.

HADROSAURUS
HAD-ro-SAW-russ *(HOW YOU PRONOUNCE MY NAME)*

- **MY FAVORITE FOOD** — Plants
- **HOW MUCH I WEIGH** — Four tons
- **HOW BIG I AM** — Twenty-six feet in length
- **HOW BIG I AM COMPARED TO YOU** — I'm the size of a killer whale
- **REGION I LIVED IN** — The US
- **ABOUT ME** — I was the first hadrosaur to be discovered, which is why they named the group after me! Like other hadrosaurs, I have a duckbill beak with no teeth. My teeth are all in my cheeks and I use them to grind up my food.

DID YOU KNOW?

There is some debate over whether Pachycephalosaurus is more closely related to the ornithopods or to the ceratopsians. Many scientists have placed it in its own group: the pachycephalosaurs.

HYPSILOPHODON
HIP-sih-LOAF-oh-don *HOW YOU PRONOUNCE MY NAME*

- **MY FAVORITE FOOD** — Plants
- **HOW MUCH I WEIGH** — Fifty-five pounds
- **HOW BIG I AM** — Six-and-a-half feet in length
- **HOW BIG I AM COMPARED TO YOU** — The size of a large pig
- **REGION I LIVED IN** — The UK and Spain
- **ABOUT ME** — I'm small but this means I can dart quickly between the trees of my woodland habitat. My eyes are on the sides of my head, which gives me good all around vision so I can spot predators that are trying to creep up on me. I run away surprisingly fast on my strong back legs.

HETERODONTOSAURUS
HET-er-o-DONT-uh-SAW-russ *HOW YOU PRONOUNCE MY NAME*

- **MY FAVORITE FOOD** — Plants and insects
- **HOW MUCH I WEIGH** — Twenty-two pounds
- **HOW BIG I AM** — Four feet in length
- **HOW BIG I AM COMPARED TO YOU** — About the size of a fox
- **REGION I LIVED IN** — Lesotho and South Africa
- **ABOUT ME** — I'm a small dinosaur but I'm full of surprises. I have three kinds of teeth, just like modern mammals do. Scientists think I probably ate insects and small rodents as well as plants, which makes me an omnivore – unusual for an ornithopod! My skin was covered in bristles, but some think it may have had feathers too.

WATCH THIS!
THE CUTEST DINOSAUR

SCAN WITH YOUR PHONE OR TABLET
https://bit.ly/3xjhHC4

WORD SCRAMBLE
Unscramble the words to spell out some dinosaur features

1. KBDCLILU
2. RUSADOARH
3. BRIOREEHV
4. ABKE
5. RDSEH
6. SETSRC

DID YOU KNOW?
The first-ever dinosaur skeleton to be mounted for display was the Hadrosaurus.

ANSWERS: 1. Duckbill 2. Hadrosaur 3. Herbivore 4. Beak 5. Herds 6. Crests

ORNITHOPOD DINOSAURS

IGUANODON
ig-WAH-no-don *(HOW YOU PRONOUNCE MY NAME)*

- **MY FAVORITE FOOD** Plants
- **HOW MUCH I WEIGH** Eight tons
- **HOW BIG I AM** Forty feet in length
- **HOW BIG I AM COMPARED TO YOU** The size of a speedboat
- **REGION I LIVED IN** Belgium and the UK
- **ABOUT ME** I am a big ornithopod with strong back legs and long arms that I use to walk on all fours when I want to. My thumb spikes are great for tearing leaves from plants – and they're a pretty good defensive weapon too!

LAMBEOSAURUS
LAM-bee-oh-SAW-russ *(HOW YOU PRONOUNCE MY NAME)*

- **MY FAVORITE FOOD** Plants
- **HOW MUCH I WEIGH** Three tons
- **HOW BIG I AM** Twenty-four feet in length
- **HOW BIG I AM COMPARED TO YOU** A little bigger than a great white shark
- **REGION I LIVED IN** Canada
- **ABOUT ME** With my duckbill beak, it's obvious I'm a hadrosaur, but I'm unique. I'm the only hadrosaur with a double-pronged head crest. My special crest helps me attract a mate.

LEAELLYNASAURA
lee-ELL-in-uh-SAW-ruh *(HOW YOU PRONOUNCE MY NAME)*

- **MY FAVORITE FOOD** Plants
- **HOW MUCH I WEIGH** Eighteen pounds
- **HOW BIG I AM** Four feet in length
- **HOW BIG I AM COMPARED TO YOU** About as long as you are tall
- **REGION I LIVED IN** Australia
- **ABOUT ME** I was found in Australia, but back when I was alive that land was close to the South Pole. I am covered in feathers which help me survive the cold temperatures, and my big eyes help me see in the dim light.

LURDUSAURUS
LUR-du-SAW-russ *(HOW YOU PRONOUNCE MY NAME)*

- **MY FAVORITE FOOD** Plants
- **HOW MUCH I WEIGH** Six tons
- **HOW BIG I AM** Thirty feet in length
- **HOW BIG I AM COMPARED TO YOU** The length of two hippos, but taller
- **REGION I LIVED IN** Niger
- **ABOUT ME** I'm bulkier than most ornithopods, with a big body, short legs, and a long neck. I have large thumb spikes which are good for fighting off predators. Scientists think my unusual shape suggests I spend most of my time in water, a bit like a hippo.

MAIASAURA

MY-ah-SAW-ah *(HOW YOU PRONOUNCE MY NAME)*

MY FAVORITE FOOD Plants
HOW MUCH I WEIGH Four tons
HOW BIG I AM Thirty feet in length
HOW BIG I AM COMPARED TO YOU
I'm as long as one-and-a-half giraffes lying down.
REGION I LIVED IN The US
ABOUT ME
Like most other hadrosaurs, I travel in a herd with my fellow Maiasaura. We roam great distances searching for the best grazing areas, but we always return to same place when it's time to nest. Our babies are weak and we need to protect them until they can run faster and find their own food.

MUTTABURRASAURUS

MUH-tah-Buh-ruh-SAW-russ *(HOW YOU PRONOUNCE MY NAME)*

MY FAVORITE FOOD Plants
HOW MUCH I WEIGH Three tons
HOW BIG I AM Twenty-three feet in length
HOW BIG I AM COMPARED TO YOU
I'm about as long as two cars
REGION I LIVED IN Australia
ABOUT ME
I have an unusual bony crest on top of my round snout. Scientists think there is an inflatable sac on this crest that makes my calls louder. My sharp beak rips plants from the ground, while my blade-like back teeth help to cut the plants up.

PACHYCEPHALOSAURUS

PACK-ee-SEFF-ah-lo-SAW-russ *(HOW YOU PRONOUNCE MY NAME)*

MY FAVORITE FOOD Plants and small animals
HOW MUCH I WEIGH 1,102 pounds
HOW BIG I AM Sixteen feet in length
HOW BIG I AM COMPARED TO YOU
I'm as long as a canoe
REGION I LIVED IN Canada and the US
ABOUT ME
I'm not very big for a dinosaur, but don't mess with me. My head is topped with spiky horns. My skull is very thick and made from a special type of bone that heals fast. During battle I use my bony skull to headbutt my opponent.

PARASAUROLOPHUS

PA-ra-SAW-ro-LOAF-uss *(HOW YOU PRONOUNCE MY NAME)*

MY FAVORITE FOOD Plants
HOW MUCH I WEIGH Three-and-a-half tons
HOW BIG I AM Thirty-three feet in length
HOW BIG I AM COMPARED TO YOU
I'm the size of four horses
REGION I LIVED IN Canada and the US
ABOUT ME
Look at my head crest – it's as long as a guitar and it makes my calls extra loud. It helps me communicate with my herd. I walk on two legs, but I can also walk on four, which is useful when I'm searching for low plants on the ground.

ORNITHOPOD DINOSAURS

HAVE YOU GOT A HADROSAUR?

Which of these ornithopods is a hadrosaur? Hadrosaurs have duckbill beaks, and some have crests

A SAUROLOPHUS

B MUTTABURRASAURUS

C LAMBEOSAURUS

D EDMONTOSAURUS

E HETERODONTOSAURUS

F ALTIRHINUS

ANSWERS: A, C, D

SHANTUNGOSAURUS
shan-TUNG-oh-SAW-russ *(HOW YOU PRONOUNCE MY NAME)*

- **MY FAVORITE FOOD** Plants
- **HOW MUCH I WEIGH** Eighteen tons
- **HOW BIG I AM** Fifty-two feet in length
- **HOW BIG I AM COMPARED TO YOU** As big as a sperm whale
- **REGION I LIVED IN** China
- **ABOUT ME** I'm the biggest ornithopod. My legs are very strong, so they can support my weight. I live in a herd and we explore the plains and swamps to find food with our duckbill beaks. I like living in a herd because it makes it harder for predators to attack.

DID YOU KNOW?
Iguanodon was named in 1825 – it was one of the first dinosaurs to be named.

SAUROLOPHUS
saw-roh-LOAF-uss *(HOW YOU PRONOUNCE MY NAME)*

- **MY FAVORITE FOOD** Plants
- **HOW MUCH I WEIGH** Three tons
- **HOW BIG I AM** Thirty feet in length
- **HOW BIG I AM COMPARED TO YOU** I'm as long as two crocodiles
- **REGION I LIVED IN** Mongolia and Canada
- **ABOUT ME** I have a bony crest on my head that grows bigger as I get older. I also have a row of spikes down my back and tail. I have hundreds of cheek teeth that help me grind my food.

TENONTOSAURUS
teh-NONT-o-SAW-russ *(HOW YOU PRONOUNCE MY NAME)*

- **MY FAVORITE FOOD** Plants
- **HOW MUCH I WEIGH** One-and-a-half tons
- **HOW BIG I AM** Twenty-six feet in length
- **HOW BIG I AM COMPARED TO YOU** As long as two large rhinos
- **REGION I LIVED IN** Canada and the US
- **ABOUT ME** I'm big and heavy, which means I move slowly. My super long tail helps me balance. It is as long as the rest of my body. Predators such as Deinonychus often attack me. I will rear up on my back legs to defend myself, but I'm too slow to escape.

END OF CHAPTER: PUZZLES & ACTIVITIES

PUT YOUR ORNITHOPOD KNOWLEDGE TO THE TEST WITH THESE PUZZLES AND ACTIVITIES

SHADOW SHAPES

Do you have dinosaur models? Trace around their shadows to compare their shapes. What features can you spot? Do they help you identify the type of dinosaur? Can you see any head crests, spikes, or other familiar features?

DINO SHOW

Put on a light show about ornithopods using a torch or a lamp and your favorite dinosaur models. Don't have dinosaur models? Create your own shadow puppets by cutting out paper or cardboard.

WATCH THIS!
SEE THE FIRST FOSSIL EVER IDENTIFIED AS A DINOSAUR

SCAN WITH YOUR PHONE OR TABLET
https://bit.ly/3wPvFVt

WATCH THIS!
MEET THE MUTTABURRASAURUS

SCAN WITH YOUR PHONE OR TABLET
https://bit.ly/374WUXB

LOST LAMBEOSAURUS

Help the lost Lambeosaurus find its way back to the herd

END OF CHAPTER: **PUZZLES & ACTIVITIES**

THINK ABOUT IT

Ornithopods weren't the biggest dinosaurs, or the fiercest. They weren't covered in armor or equipped with defensive weapons. So why did the ornithopods thrive so well? Discuss with your friends!

TRUE OR FALSE?

ALL ORNITHOPODS ARE HADROSAURS
TRUE ☐ OR FALSE ☐

SOME ORNITHOPODS MAY HAVE BEEN MEAT-EATERS TOO
TRUE ☐ OR FALSE ☐

ORNITHOPODS HAD NO CLAWS, SPIKES, OR HORNS
TRUE ☐ OR FALSE ☐

DENTAL BATTERIES GAVE ORNITHOPODS EXTRA ENERGY
TRUE ☐ OR FALSE ☐

ORNITHOPODS ARE CLOSELY RELATED TO THE CERATOPSIANS
TRUE ☐ OR FALSE ☐

ANSWERS: False, true, false, false, true

MAIASAURA MATH

A large number of Maiasaura nests, eggs, and young Maiasaura fossils have been found at a site in Montana which is now known as Egg Mountain. If there were ten Maiasaura nests, and half of them contained fifteen eggs while the other half contained sixteen eggs, how many eggs would there be?

ANSWER: 155

COMPLETE THE CAMPTOSAURUS

Some parts of the Camptosaurus are missing. Can you complete the picture?

WHAT HAVE YOU LEARNED?

1 WHAT WAS THE LARGEST ORNITHOPOD?

2 WHERE DID SOME ORNITHOPODS HAVE A SPIKE?

3 WHICH ORNITHOPOD HAD A DOUBLE-PRONGED HEAD CREST?

4 WHAT WERE THE ROWS OF TEETH IN A HADROSAURS" CHEEKS CALLED?

5 WHICH ORNITHOPOD LIVED CLOSE TO THE SOUTH POLE?

6 ORNITHOPODS WERE THE _____ OF THE PREHISTORIC WORLD

7 WHICH ORNITHOPOD HAS BEEN COMPARED TO A HIPPO?

8 WHEN DID THE FIRST ORNITHOPODS LIVE?

9 DID ALL HADROSAURS HAVE A HEAD CREST?

LATE TRIASSIC PERIOD · ALTIRHINUS · BEAK · COWS · CRETACEOUS PERIOD · DENTAL BATTERY · EDMONTOSAURUS · FROGS · IGUANODON · JURASSIC PERIOD · LAMBEOSAURUS · LEAELLYNASAURA · LIONS · LURDUSAURUS · MAIASAURA · MAYBE · MUTTABURRASAURUS · NO · NOSE · ORNITHOPOD · PACHYCEPHALOSAURUS · PARASAUROLOPHUS · SHANTUNGOSAURUS · SHEARING TEETH · TAIL · THUMB · YES

ANSWERS: 1. Shantungosaurus 2. Thumb 3. Lambeosaurus 4. Dental battery 5. Leaellynasaura 6. Cows 7. Lurdusaurus 8. Late Triassic period 9. No

ORNITHOPOD LINE UP

Can you put these ornithopods in size order? Label the smallest A and the largest E

1  EDMONTOSAURUS

2 ALTIRHINUS

3  SHANTUNGOSAURUS

4  HETERODONTOSAURUS

5  LURDUSAURUS

ANSWERS: 1D, 2B, 3E, 4A, 5C

DRAW A DRYOSAURUS

Can you draw a Dryosaurus?

58

END OF CHAPTER: PUZZLES & ACTIVITIES

WORD WHEEL

How many words can you find in the word wheel that relate to ornithopods?

ORNITHOPOD PHOTOGRAPHY

Can you create a realistic-looking dinosaur scene to capture some photos of ornithopods in the wild? Think about props you can use or find a leafy location for your dinosaurs to explore.

WATCH THIS!
WHAT DID PARASAUROLOPHUS REALLY SOUND LIKE?

SCAN WITH YOUR PHONE OR TABLET

https://bit.ly/3DsqKl8

PARASAUROLOPHUS PUZZLE

Using the numbers, piece the Parasaurolophus puzzle together

59

LONG-NECKED DINOSAURS

Sauropods are the big ones – the gigantic, long-necked dinosaurs that stomped through the Late Jurassic and Cretaceous world, munching away on leaves and plants. Their immense size and long, flexible necks meant they could reach the leaves of the tallest trees, but their huge bodies made them slow. Predators could easily outrun sauropods, but who would win in a fight? Sauropods had tough, scaly skin, and some of them were so enormous that predators wouldn't even bother to attack. However, if a predator did come close, sauropods would use the one weapon they had: their tails. Long and slender, sauropod tails had two functions – to help balance those huge, heavy necks, and to whip sharply at approaching predators. A swish from a sauropod tail would be powerful enough to break a few T-Rex bones for sure.

Sauropods spent their time grazing. Their huge bodies needed a lot of food to keep going, so sauropods pretty much spent all day eating. They didn't need to think about much else, so they had quite small heads, and even smaller brains. Their teeth were adapted for tearing and grinding up leaves and tough plant matter. Many sauropods, including Giraffatitan, had spoon-shaped teeth which were perfect for stripping leaves from branches. Others, such as Amargasaurus, had pencil-like teeth which were good for slicing through plants.

Sauropods walked on four legs, but many of them could rear up on their hind legs against a tree to reach even higher. To help with this, their legs were strong and sturdy, and many had an inwards-facing claw on their front legs which they could use to grip onto a tree trunk. Sauropod feet were wide and round. This shape helped stop heavy sauropods from sinking into the ground. There are several sites around the world where sauropod footprints have been preserved to this day.

SPOT THE DIFFERENCE

Find five differences between these two pictures

I SPY A SAUROPOD

Can you find two sauropods in these pictures?

ANSWERS: A, E

LONG-NECKED DINOSAURS

WATCH THIS!
THE BIGGEST DINOSAUR
SCAN WITH YOUR PHONE OR TABLET
https://bit.ly/3uUtu6M

DID YOU KNOW?
Sauropods were all bigger than the land animals that are alive today. But they ranged in length from twenty feet to a whopping 115 feet!

WHAT MAKES A SAUROPOD DINOSAUR?

- ✓ Plant-eater
- ✓ Walked on four legs
- ✓ Long neck
- ✓ Small head
- ✓ Long tail
- ✓ Wide, round feet

SAUROPOD DINOSAURS

There are three main groups of sauropods, each with different features: brachiosaurids, diplodocoids, and titanosaurids. Brachiosaurids had thinner necks than most other sauropods, and they were also exceptionally long in comparison to their body size. Their front legs were significantly taller than their hind legs, which meant their backs sloped down to their tails. Brachiosaurids include Brachiosaurus, as well as Giraffatitan. Diplodocoids are massive dinosaurs, but they are a bit more slender than the stocky, sturdy brachiosaurids and titanosaurids. Diplodocoids have four short legs. Their front legs are slightly shorter than their back legs, so their backs dip a little before the neck begins. Experts don't think diplodocoids could raise their necks as high as the other sauropods, so they probably fed on lower tree branches or used their necks to reach out into marshes or dense clumps of trees. Diplodocoids include Diplodocus, Supersaurus, and Apatosaurus. Titanosaurids were the last remaining type of sauropods at the time of the asteroid and included all the truly enormous sauropods. However, although the word "titanosaurid" comes from the Titans of the Greek myths, not all titanosaurids were huge. Titanosaurids include the enormous Argentinosaurus and the small Magyarosaurus.

AMARGASAURUS
ah-MAR-gah-SAW-russ *(HOW YOU PRONOUNCE MY NAME)*

- **MY FAVORITE FOOD** — Plants and leaves
- **HOW MUCH I WEIGH** — Three tons
- **HOW BIG I AM** — Thirty-one feet in length
- **HOW BIG I AM COMPARED TO YOU** — I am about as tall as an ostrich
- **REGION I LIVED IN** — Argentina
- **ABOUT ME** — I'm a sauropod with a difference – I have a double row of spines along my neck and back. The neck spines are pretty big and support a neck sail, which I use to scare off predators and attract a mate.

WORD SEARCH
Can you find all of these words?

```
J A B T L K O D S B N H I L A S
O H G E R N K L A E R F B G H O
B I O G S A U R U N J K I R G D
A U R N G R E Q R I L P Z A R I
R S D G N J L I O A R V H M L P
I A L T D B H L P E S R T Y N L
A R T S A U R U O V L O P A S O
L E A V E S T F D G B L E A Y D
E H G R B L K P O B S N V D R O
A R B H A D R T H J A E J K L C
G S U P E R S A U R U S E R G U
H A R G V N L A S R S A U R N S
M R T A J K U E D B H L P R H Y
K C E G Y U H E R B I V O R E T
N E C K S A R U I L P R A B H M
```

NECK · **LEAVES** · **HERBIVORE** · **JOBARIA** · **SUPERSAURUS** · **DIPLODOCUS** · **SAUROPOD**

ANTARCTOSAURUS
ant-ARK-toe-SAW-russ *(HOW YOU PRONOUNCE MY NAME)*

- **MY FAVORITE FOOD** — Leaves and plants
- **HOW MUCH I WEIGH** — Thirty-seven tons
- **HOW BIG I AM** — Fifty-nine feet in length
- **HOW BIG I AM COMPARED TO YOU** — I am as long as three great white sharks
- **REGION I LIVED IN** — Argentina, Chile, Uruguay
- **ABOUT ME** — Not many of my remains have been found, so scientists are a bit confused about what I looked like. They have found two of my huge thigh bones, though, which measure eight feet long – that's almost as long as a giraffe's neck.

SAUROPOD DINOSAURS

APATOSAURUS
a-PAT-oh-SAW-russ
(HOW YOU PRONOUNCE MY NAME)

- **MY FAVORITE FOOD** — Leaves and plants
- **HOW MUCH I WEIGH** — Thirty-three tons
- **HOW BIG I AM** — Eighty-two feet in length
- **HOW BIG I AM COMPARED TO YOU** — I'm the length of a bowling alley
- **REGION I LIVED IN** — The US
- **ABOUT ME** — My four sturdy legs help support my enormous body as I slowly stomp around searching for food. My tail helps me balance and is also a whip-like weapon against predators.

ARGENTINOSAURUS
AR-jen-TEEN-o-SAW-russ
(HOW YOU PRONOUNCE MY NAME)

- **MY FAVORITE FOOD** — Plants and the uppermost leaves
- **HOW MUCH I WEIGH** — Seventy-seven tons
- **HOW BIG I AM** — 115 feet in length
- **HOW BIG I AM COMPARED TO YOU** — Massive – even my footprint would be bigger than a twelve year old
- **REGION I LIVED IN** — Argentina
- **ABOUT ME** — I'm enormous, even for a titanosaurid. I am a very slow walker, but that doesn't bother me. I take my time going from one tree to the next, eating constantly. I need to eat around 1 ton of plant matter a day.

DID YOU KNOW?
Argentinosaurus is perhaps the largest land animal that ever lived.

ATLASAURUS
AT-lass-SAW-russ
(HOW YOU PRONOUNCE MY NAME)

- **MY FAVORITE FOOD** — Leaves and plants
- **HOW MUCH I WEIGH** — Fifteen tons
- **HOW BIG I AM** — Forty-nine feet in length
- **HOW BIG I AM COMPARED TO YOU** — I am taller than a telephone pole
- **REGION I LIVED IN** — Africa
- **ABOUT ME** — My front legs are longer than my back legs, so my back slopes downwards like Brachiosaurus, although I am about half the size. Having longer front legs means I can run faster than most other sauropods.

BRACHIOSAURUS
brack-ee-o-SAW-russ
(HOW YOU PRONOUNCE MY NAME)

- **MY FAVORITE FOOD** — Leaves and plants
- **HOW MUCH I WEIGH** — Thirty-three tons
- **HOW BIG I AM** — Seventy-five feet in length
- **HOW BIG I AM COMPARED TO YOU** — As tall as a three-story building
- **REGION I LIVED IN** — Algeria, Portugal, Tanzania, and the US
- **ABOUT ME** — I'm famous for my long neck – it's more than half the length of my whole body. I have tall front legs and short back legs, so my neck can reach the very high branches on trees where the best leaves are.

BRONTOMERUS
bron-TOE-meh-russ *(HOW YOU PRONOUNCE MY NAME)*

MY FAVORITE FOOD — Plants and leaves
HOW MUCH I WEIGH — Seven tons
HOW BIG I AM — Forty-six feet in length
HOW BIG I AM COMPARED TO YOU
I'm as tall as five ten-year-old kids standing one on top of the other
REGION I LIVED IN — North America
ABOUT ME
Like most other sauropods, I have a long neck, a long tail, and a small brain. I am very proud of my thigh muscles, though, because they are super strong. I can even use my hind legs to kick out at predators if they dare come too close.

BRONTOSAURUS
bron-toe-SAW-russ *(HOW YOU PRONOUNCE MY NAME)*

MY FAVORITE FOOD — Leaves and plants
HOW MUCH I WEIGH — Sixteen and a half tons
HOW BIG I AM — Seventy-two feet in length
HOW BIG I AM COMPARED TO YOU
I'm as long as three reticulated pythons – the longest snake in the world
REGION I LIVED IN — The US
ABOUT ME
I look like a very typical sauropod: long neck, sturdy legs, and a long tail. I can reach high up on the trees to find the best leaves, which I digest in my big stomach. My tail is thinner than most sauropods, which means it makes a loud crack when I whip it.

DICRAEOSAURUS
DIH-cray-oh-SAW-russ *(HOW YOU PRONOUNCE MY NAME)*

MY FAVORITE FOOD — Leaves and plants
HOW MUCH I WEIGH — Seven tons
HOW BIG I AM — Forty-five feet in length
HOW BIG I AM COMPARED TO YOU
I'm as long as three giraffes
REGION I LIVED IN — Tanzania
ABOUT ME
I'm small for a sauropod, but I'm still bigger than most of my predators. A row of double-forked spikes runs down my back and tail, which is how I got my name – it means 'double-forked lizard."

DIPLODOCUS
dip-LOD-o-kuss *(HOW YOU PRONOUNCE MY NAME)*

MY FAVORITE FOOD — Plants and the highest leaves on the tree
HOW MUCH I WEIGH — Sixteen and a half tons
HOW BIG I AM — Eighty-five feet in length
HOW BIG I AM COMPARED TO YOU
Almost as big as a blue whale
REGION I LIVED IN — The US
ABOUT ME
I'm simply enormous. I tower over all the other dinosaurs I see. My huge body needs so much food for fuel that I pretty much eat all day long. My long tail balances out my long neck so I don't fall over.

DID YOU KNOW?
Scientists are still arguing about whether Brontosaurus and Apatosaurus are the same species.

SAUROPOD DINOSAURS

DID YOU KNOW?
Brachiosaurid teeth were shaped like a spoon, whereas diplodocoid teeth were pencil or peg shaped. Titanosaurid teeth were a mix of the two.

EUROPASAURUS
yoo-ROE-pa-SAW-russ *(HOW YOU PRONOUNCE MY NAME)*

- **MY FAVORITE FOOD** Leaves and plants
- **HOW MUCH I WEIGH** 1,700 pounds
- **HOW BIG I AM** Twenty feet in length
- **HOW BIG I AM COMPARED TO YOU** I'm as big as a bull
- **REGION I LIVED IN** Germany
- **ABOUT ME** I'm small for a sauropod. In fact, I'm one of the smallest species. Some scientists call me a mini-sauropod. But I still have a long neck, which is flexible enough to reach both tall trees and low plants.

GIRAFFATITAN
ji-RAHF-a-TIE-tan *(HOW YOU PRONOUNCE MY NAME)*

- **MY FAVORITE FOOD** Plants and the uppermost leaves
- **HOW MUCH I WEIGH** Twenty-eight tons
- **HOW BIG I AM** Seventy-two feet in length
- **HOW BIG I AM COMPARED TO YOU** You'd need to stand on the ladder of a fire engine to see me face to face
- **REGION I LIVED IN** Tanzania
- **ABOUT ME** My amazingly long neck makes up half the length of my body. My neck bones are hollow, which is the only way it can stay up. I don't need to rear up on my hind legs to reach the topmost branches – my neck is long enough.

JOBARIA
joe-BAR-REE-ah *(HOW YOU PRONOUNCE MY NAME)*

- **MY FAVORITE FOOD** Leaves and plants
- **HOW MUCH I WEIGH** Twenty tons
- **HOW BIG I AM** Sixty-six feet in length
- **HOW BIG I AM COMPARED TO YOU** I can reach up to the third floor of a building
- **REGION I LIVED IN** Niger
- **ABOUT ME** My neck is quite short for a sauropod, but luckily my hind legs can support my full body weight, so I can stand up against tree trunks to reach the higher leaves.

MAGYAROSAURUS
mag-YAR-o-SAW-russ *(HOW YOU PRONOUNCE MY NAME)*

- **MY FAVORITE FOOD** Leaves and plants
- **HOW MUCH I WEIGH** One ton
- **HOW BIG I AM** Sixteen feet in length
- **HOW BIG I AM COMPARED TO YOU** I am the size of a large car
- **REGION I LIVED IN** Romania
- **ABOUT ME** I'm very small for a sauropod, but because I lived on an island there were very few predators to defend myself from. My size means I can still reach some leaves, but I also eat low-lying plants from the ground as well.

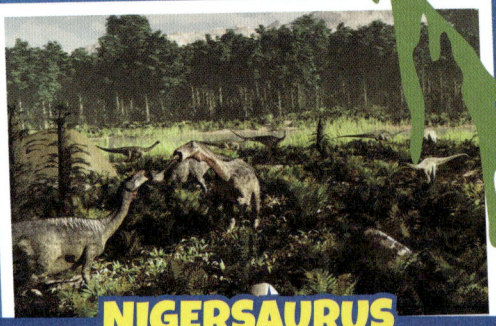

MAMENCHISAURUS

ma-MEN-chee-SAW-russ *HOW YOU PRONOUNCE MY NAME*

MY FAVORITE FOOD Leaves and plants

HOW MUCH I WEIGH Thirty-nine tons

HOW BIG I AM Eighty-five feet in length

HOW BIG I AM COMPARED TO YOU
My legs are as big as tree trunks and my neck is as long as a double-decker bus

REGION I LIVED IN China

ABOUT ME
It's obvious that I have an exceptionally long neck. But I'm proud to tell you that I have the longest neck of any animal ever. This means I can reach the highest leaves on the trees.

NIGERSAURUS

NY-juh-SAW-russ *HOW YOU PRONOUNCE MY NAME*

MY FAVORITE FOOD Leaves and plants

HOW MUCH I WEIGH Four tons

HOW BIG I AM Thirty feet in length

HOW BIG I AM COMPARED TO YOU
I'm about as tall as an elephant

REGION I LIVED IN
Algeria, Niger, and Tunisia

ABOUT ME
I'm a small sauropod, but take a look at my face to see what makes me stand out. My snout and jaws are wide and straight-edged. When I'm grazing, I sweep my neck back and forth to tear off the plants in front of me.

SAUROPOSEIDON

SAW-ro-po-SY-den *HOW YOU PRONOUNCE MY NAME*

MY FAVORITE FOOD
The very uppermost leaves on the tallest trees

HOW MUCH I WEIGH Sixty-six tons

HOW BIG I AM 105 feet in length

HOW BIG I AM COMPARED TO YOU
I am as tall as three giraffes

REGION I LIVED IN North America

ABOUT ME
Once I have fully grown, I'm safe from most predators thanks to my immense size. I have my pick of the tastiest leaves at the top of the trees because even most other sauropods can't reach them.

SHUNOSAURUS

SHOO-noe-SAW-russ *HOW YOU PRONOUNCE MY NAME*

MY FAVORITE FOOD Leaves and plants

HOW MUCH I WEIGH Four tons

HOW BIG I AM Thirty-three feet in length

HOW BIG I AM COMPARED TO YOU
I'm a bit bigger than a double-decker bus

REGION I LIVED IN China

ABOUT ME
I have a secret weapon. Most sauropods use their tails to whip at predators. But my tail has spikes on the end, so I bash at my predators too. My tail spikes help keep them away so I can continue munching on delicious leaves.

DID YOU KNOW?

There's a cast of a Diplodocus skeleton at the Natural History Museum in London. It has 292 bones and is nicknamed Dippy.

SAUROPOD DINOSAURS

SPINOPHOROSAURUS
SPINE-oh-foro-SAW-russ *HOW YOU PRONOUNCE MY NAME*

MY FAVORITE FOOD Leaves and plants
HOW MUCH I WEIGH Seven tons
HOW BIG I AM Forty-three feet in length
HOW BIG I AM COMPARED TO YOU I'm as long as two elephants
REGION I LIVED IN Niger

ABOUT ME
I'm one of the earlier sauropods, but I'm pretty big compared to the others who lived at the same time as me. I stand on my hind legs to reach the highest tree branches and then I use my peg-like teeth to pull off leaves, which I swallow whole.

TRUE OR FALSE?

ALL TITANOSAURIDS ARE ENORMOUS
TRUE ☐ OR FALSE ☐

ANTARCTOSAURUS LIVED IN ANTARCTICA
TRUE ☐ OR FALSE ☐

ALL SAUROPODS HAVE SMALL BRAINS
TRUE ☐ OR FALSE ☐

ANSWERS: False, false, true.

BALANCING ACT

Sauropod bodies evolved in a way that allowed their enormous necks to be supported – otherwise they would have just toppled over because their necks were too heavy. Their tails helped balance their weight and their neck bones were hollow, supporting the neck without making it too heavy. Try building a simple sauropod-like model. Can you get the balance just right to keep it standing?

WHAT YOU'LL NEED
- Cardboard tubes
- Toothpicks
- Tape
- Pencils

INSTRUCTIONS
1. Turn the cardboard tube into a sauropod body by adding four toothpick legs. Secure these with tape as necessary.
2. Attach a pencil where the neck would go. Make sure it points forwards, not up.
3. Can you attach another pencil as a tail to help your sauropod balance? You might have to experiment with pencils of different sizes and weights, or even try attaching them to the body at different angles.

SUPERSAURUS
SOO-per-SAW-russ *HOW YOU PRONOUNCE MY NAME*

MY FAVORITE FOOD Leaves and plants
HOW MUCH I WEIGH Forty-four tons
HOW BIG I AM 115 feet in length
HOW BIG I AM COMPARED TO YOU As big as a wing on a jumbo jet!
REGION I LIVED IN The US and Europe

ABOUT ME
I'm one of the largest land animals ever – experts are uncertain who was bigger: me or Argentinosaurus. My neck is thinner than Argentinosaurus and I have a line of small spikes going all the way down my back and tail.

END OF CHAPTER: PUZZLES & ACTIVITIES

LET'S TEST YOUR SAUROPOD KNOWLEDGE

MAKE YOUR OWN DINOSAUR EGGS

Several fossilized Apatosaurus eggs have been discovered. Each egg is about as big as a basketball. That's big compared to chicken eggs, but quite small considering the size of an Apatosaurus. It tells us that dinosaurs probably grew quite quickly once they were born. Let's make our own dinosaur eggs with hard-boiled eggs and vinegar using a scientific method known as acid dye. Acid helps food coloring scheckmark to surfaces, so when we soak the eggs in vinegar, the acid from the vinegar helps the food coloring scheckmark to the shell.

WHAT YOU'LL NEED

- Cooled hard-boiled eggs
- Heat-resistant bowls or cups
- Hot water
- Vinegar
- Food coloring
- Spoon
- Paint
- Glitter

INSTRUCTIONS

1. Pour about half a cup of hot water into each of your bowls. You might want to ask an adult to help with this.
2. Add two tablespoons of vinegar and several drops of food coloring to each bowl. Use a different bowl for each different color.
3. Place a hard-boiled egg into each bowl and leave it for at least five minutes. You might want to turn the egg over halfway through so it dyes evenly.
4. Use a spoon to remove the eggs from the bowls. Leave them to dry for about ten minutes.
5. Now your eggs should be beautifully colored with your chosen dye. Add paint and glitter to create your own unique dinosaur eggs – which dinosaur would your beautiful eggs belong to?

WHICH SAUROPOD AM I?

Can you name the sauropod?

I HAVE DOUBLE-FORKED SPIKES DOWN MY BACK

I HAVE THE LONGEST NECK OF ALL

I AM CALLED A MINI-SAUROPOD

I HAVE A NECK SAIL

I HAVE EXCEPTIONALLY STRONG THIGH MUSCLES

I HAVE SPIKES ON THE END OF MY TAIL

ANSWERS: Dicraeosaurus, Mamenchisaurus, Europasaurus, Amargasaurus, Brontomerus, Shunosaurus

ARRANGE THE ANTARCTOSAURUS

Can you arrange the pieces of Antarctosaurus in the correct order?

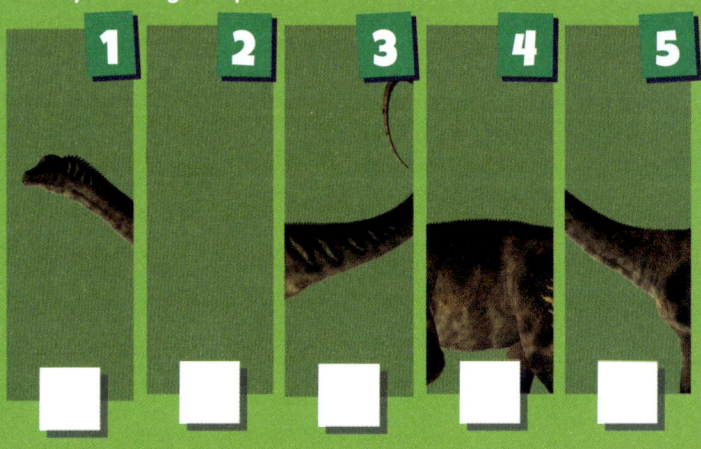

ANSWERS: 1A, 2E, 3D, 4C, 5B.

END OF CHAPTER: **PUZZLES & ACTIVITIES**

COUNT THE SAUROPODS

There are lots of sauropods in this box. Count how many of each you can spot

ANSWERS: 12, 11, 8

TRY IT OUT

Grab a watch, timer, or stopwatch and time yourself for sixty seconds: can you talk about sauropods for a whole minute? Ready, steady, go!

QUIZ

HOW MUCH DO YOU KNOW ABOUT SAUROPODS?

WHAT HELPS A SAUROPOD SUPPORT ITS NECK?
A. Wide, round feet
B. Hollow bones
C. Tiny brain

WHAT SAUROPOD FEATURE HELPS GRIP A TREE WHEN TRYING TO REACH FOR HIGH-UP LEAVES?
A: Spoon-like teeth
B: Grappling hook
C: Claws on its front feet

WHICH GROUP OF SAUROPODS DOES MAGYAROSAURUS BELONG TO?
A: Brachiosaurids
B: Diplodocoids
C: Titanosaurids

WHICH SAUROPOD HAS AN UNUSUAL FACE WITH WIDE, STRAIGHT-EDGED JAWS?
A: Nigersaurus
B: Dicraeosaurus
C: Europasaurus

SCIENTISTS CAN'T DECIDE WHETHER WHICH TWO SAUROPODS ARE THE SAME SPECIES OR NOT?
A: Brachiosaurus and Mamenchisaurus
B: Apatosaurus and Brontosaurus
C: Supersaurus and Sauroposeidon

ANSWERS: B, C, C, A, B

FIND THE TASTIEST TREE

This Giraffatitan is hungry! Help them find the best tree in the forest by working out the math problems and moving them around the grid

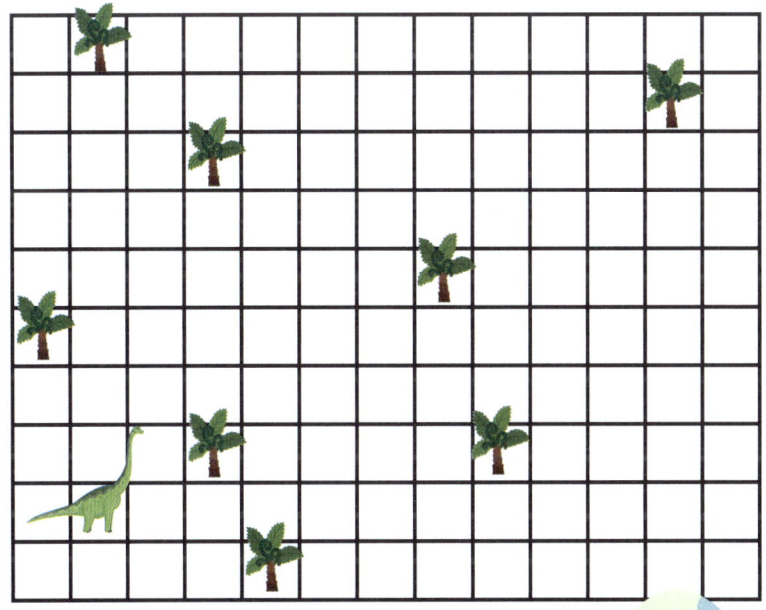

1. Go right 3 x ☐ = 27
2. Go up 48 ÷ 24 = ☐
3. Go left 25 ÷ 5 = ☐
4. Go up 12 x ☐ = 36
5. Go right 54 ÷ 9 = ☐
6. Go down 33 x ☐ = 66
7. Go left 77 ÷ 7 = ☐

ANSWERS: 9, 2, 5, 3, 6, 2, 11

COMPLETE THE SAUROPOD SENTENCES

1. Sauropods lived in the Late _____ and _____ periods.

   CRETACEOUS JURASSIC TRIASSIC

2. Sauropods are known for their long _____ and _____.

   TAILS TEETH NECKS ARMS CLAWS

3. _____ have spoon-shaped teeth.

   MAMENCHISAURUS DIPLODOCOIDS BRACHIOSAURIDS

4. Sauropods are so large, they need to _____ all day long.

   WALK EAT SLEEP NAP

ANSWERS: 1. Jurassic, Cretaceous 2. Necks, tails 3. Brachiosaurids 4. Eat

TRY IT OUT

Imagine you're part of a team that just discovered a skeleton that looks like the biggest sauropod of all time. It's a brand new species! Draw what it would have looked like back in the Cretaceous period and give your new dinosaur a name

WORD SCRAMBLE

Can you uncover the scrambled words?

1. OSATUPAARSU
2. SAOUNRTURBSO
3. IODUDLPCSO
4. REUUSSAPUSR
5. UANGUIEATRNROSS

ANSWERS: 1. Apatosaurus 2. Brontosaurus 3. Diplodocus 4. Supersaurus 5. Argentinosaurus

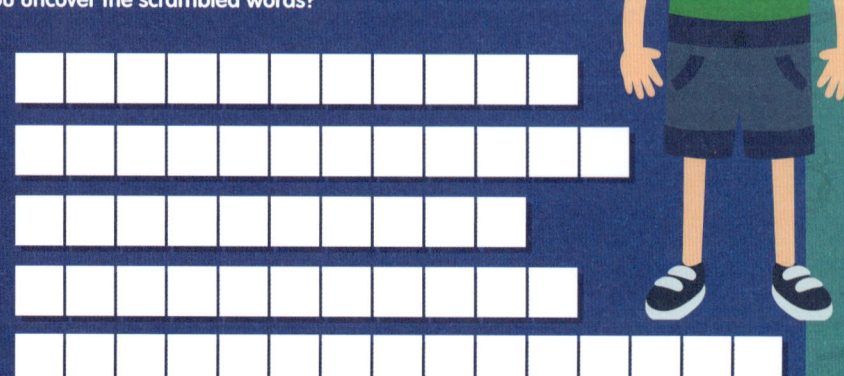

END OF CHAPTER: PUZZLES & ACTIVITIES

SAUROPOD SHADOW MATCHING

Can you match the dinosaur to its silhouette?

PAPIER-MÂCHÉ SAUROPODS

Sauropods have a very recognizable shape – especially the long neck topped with a small head. Let's build a sauropod using papier-mâché. Think about the different features of the sauropod dinosaurs and how they vary by group – the brachiosaurids, diplodocoids, and titanosaurids. Which will you choose?

WHAT YOU'LL NEED

- Cardboard
- Tape
- Old newspaper, magazines, or comics
- A mug of plain flour
- A mug of warm water
- Paints (optional)

INSTRUCTIONS

1. Build your sauropod shape using cardboard and tape. Don't worry if it doesn't look pretty – focus on getting the shape right and decorating will come later on.
2. Tear your paper into strips before you make the paste. Make plenty so that you don't need to tear more later.
3. Mix the flour and water in a bowl until there are no lumps. You want it to be the same consistency as cake batter. Add extra warm water if it's too thick – but make sure to add it slowly.
4. Dip each strip of paper in the papier-mâché mixture, wipe off excess paste and place it on your dinosaur model. You want to cover it completely.
5. Smooth the paper down using your fingers or a paintbrush. Leave each layer to dry before adding another one.
6. When you are happy with the shape and finish of your sauropod, leave it to dry completely and then paint or decorate as you like.

WHAT DID YOU LEARN?

Sauropods were huge animals. Their bodies were perfectly designed, with long tails to balance their long necks, and wide, round feet to stop them from sinking into the ground. What did you need to think about as you built your papier-mâché dinosaur? Did you need to balance its neck and tail to stop it falling over? Do you think it would stand up so well if it had thin, pointy toes?

JIGSAW

Using the numbers, piece the jigsaw puzzle together to create a picture of what might have been the largest land animal ever

MEAT-EATING DINOSAURS

Time to meet the meat-eaters! While all carnivorous dinosaurs were theropods, it's important to remember that not all theropods were carnivores. Some were omnivores – eating both meat and plants – some were insectivores, and some were herbivores. But most of them were carnivores, predators, and hunters. The main thing all theropods had in common was that they walked on two legs.

Theropods first appeared in the Late Triassic period. They started off small, like Coelophysis and Herrerasaurus, who would dart through the trees hunting for small animals. Throughout the Jurassic period, theropods evolved into lots of different groups. None were mightier than the large, fierce predators such as Allosaurus and Megalosaurus. By the time the Cretaceous period began, these powerful theropods ruled the Earth, and none more so than the mighty Tyrannosaurus.

Theropods walked on two legs, which were strong enough to support their weight and powerful enough to run quite fast. Their front legs – or arms, depending on how you look at it – grew smaller because they weren't needed for walking. Scientists think that having small arms was actually a good thing for the big predators because they didn't get in the way during a battle, so they stayed safe from injury.

Theropod feet had sharp claws, and most theropods had claws on their hands as well. A long, stiff tail helped them balance. Most theropods had sharp, serrated teeth. Serrated means they had jagged edges, like a knife. This helped cut and tear the flesh of their prey. Many theropods had feathers, too.

Famous theropods include Velociraptor, Spinosaurus, Giganotosaurus, Baryonyx, and Tyrannosaurus. They ruled the Earth for millions of years, hunting the plentiful herbivorous dinosaurs until the asteroid destroyed nearly all of them. The only dinosaurs to survive the mass extinction were a small group of theropods – the flying ones – who are now known to us as birds.

WHAT MAKES A THEROPOD DINOSAUR?

- ✓ Walked on two legs
- ✓ Most were carnivorous, but not all of them
- ✓ Strong back legs
- ✓ Three-toed feet
- ✓ Small arms
- ✓ Sharp claws
- ✓ Sharp, serrated teeth
- ✓ Stiff tail

MEAT-EATING DINOSAURS

WATCH THIS!
WHO WERE THE THEROPODS?
SCAN WITH YOUR PHONE OR TABLET
https://bit.ly/3O1jS3d

BUILT TO HUNT

Theropods evolved to be powerful and vicious carnivores. Label the features on this theropod that help it find, chase, and defeat its prey

DID YOU KNOW?

The Tyrannosaurus only appeared just before mass extinction. This carnivorous dinosaur had very short arms, but scientists are still working out why and how they were useful to this very incredible beast!

THEROPOD DINOSAURS

Theropods range from tiny, birdlike flying dinosaurs to massive, ferocious predators. There are many different groups of theropods, but let's talk about the four main groups. Ceratosaurs were the most typical theropods, while the rest evolved to be more specialized in their own environments. Ceratosaurs include Carnotaurus, Majungasaurus, and Masiakasaurus. They all have very short arms and are more likely to have horns on their heads. The other main theropod groups are the megalosaurids – including Megalosaurus and Spinosaurus – allosaurids – including Allosaurus and Mapusaurus – and coelurosaurs – the most wide-ranging group, including Tyrannosaurus, Compsognathus and the flying dinosaurs.

Theropods are mostly known as meat-eaters, but scientists have worked out that different environments caused certain groups of theropods to change their diets. Some lived near water and evolved to eat fish, such as Spinosaurus and Masiakasaurus. Others ate insects, especially smaller theropods like Sinosauropteryx and Juravenator. Other theropods were omnivorous, meaning they ate both meat and plants, such as Deinocheirus and Oviraptor. Herbivorous theropods were rare, though there were a few, including Therizinosaurus.

DID YOU KNOW?

In 1824, Megalosaurus became the first dinosaur to be given a scientific name.

ALBERTOSAURUS
al-BERT-oh-SAW-russ *(HOW YOU PRONOUNCE MY NAME)*

MY FAVORITE FOOD — Meat
HOW MUCH I WEIGH — Two tons
HOW BIG I AM — Thirty feet in length
HOW BIG I AM COMPARED TO YOU — I'm bigger than a killer whale
REGION I LIVED IN — Canada
ABOUT ME — I'm about half the size of my famous cousin Tyrannosaurus, but I'm no less fierce. My sharp, curved teeth can bite through bone. My long legs help me chase my prey quickly, and then I use my teeth to catch and kill.

THEROPOD FAMILY TREE

Can you fill in the missing theropod groups?

THEROPODS

- A: _____
  - B: _____
    - CARNOTAURUS / MAJUNGASAURUS
  - MEGALOSAURUS / SPINOSAURUS
- C: _____
  - ALLOSAURUS / MAPUSAURUS
  - D: _____
    - TYRANNOSAURUS / COMPSOGNATHUS

ANSWERS: A. Ceratosaurs B. Megalosaurids C. Allosaurids D. Coelurosaurs

THEROPOD DINOSAURS

ALLOSAURUS
al-oh-SAW-russ
HOW YOU PRONOUNCE MY NAME

- **MY FAVORITE FOOD** Meat
- **HOW MUCH I WEIGH** Two-and-a-half tons
- **HOW BIG I AM** Thirty-four feet in length
- **HOW BIG I AM COMPARED TO YOU** The size of one-and-a-half elephants
- **REGION I LIVED IN** Portugal and the US
- **ABOUT ME**

I'm one of the fiercest predators of all time. I'm fast, clever, and not afraid of anything. My jaws open wide, showing off my sharp, serrated teeth, and my razor-sharp claws are as long as a banana. Sometimes I use my head to hit my prey before I grab it.

CARNOTAURUS
kar-no-TAW-russ
HOW YOU PRONOUNCE MY NAME

- **MY FAVORITE FOOD** Meat
- **HOW MUCH I WEIGH** Two tons
- **HOW BIG I AM** Twenty-six feet in length
- **HOW BIG I AM COMPARED TO YOU** As big as two Jeeps
- **REGION I LIVED IN** Argentina
- **ABOUT ME**

I'm one of the most fearsome hunters of the Southern Hemisphere. I can run as fast as a leopard thanks to my strong leg muscles, though my arms are extremely small. My back is covered in spikes and osteoderms, and I have a line of spikes under my chin too.

COELOPHYSIS
SEE-lo-FY-siss
HOW YOU PRONOUNCE MY NAME

- **MY FAVORITE FOOD** Small animals
- **HOW MUCH I WEIGH** 100 pounds
- **HOW BIG I AM** Ten feet in length
- **HOW BIG I AM COMPARED TO YOU** The size of a big dog
- **REGION I LIVED IN** South Africa, the US and Zimbabwe
- **ABOUT ME**

I'm slim and speedy. I have excellent eyesight that helps me spot prey darting among the trees. My three-fingered hands are great for grabbing prey, and my flexible neck and long, narrow snout are perfect for reaching prey in their burrows or other crevices.

COMPSOGNATHUS
COMP-sog-NAY-thus
HOW YOU PRONOUNCE MY NAME

- **MY FAVORITE FOOD** Meat
- **HOW MUCH I WEIGH** Seven pounds
- **HOW BIG I AM** Four feet in length
- **HOW BIG I AM COMPARED TO YOU** The size of a small dog
- **REGION I LIVED IN** France and Germany
- **ABOUT ME**

I'm little but vicious. I'm a skilled predator and I hunt for small animals and dinosaur eggs in the forests of Europe. I'm covered in small feathers and I have sharp claws for capturing prey and short, pointy teeth for tearing meat.

DEINOCHEIRUS
DINE-oh-KIRE-us *(HOW YOU PRONOUNCE MY NAME)*

MY FAVORITE FOOD Meat and plants
HOW MUCH I WEIGH Seven tons
HOW BIG I AM Thirty-six feet in length
HOW BIG I AM COMPARED TO YOU Longer than two canoes
REGION I LIVED IN Mongolia
ABOUT ME
I belong to a group of theropods called ornithomimosaurs, which means I look like an anicent ostrich. I have a duck-like beak, humped back, really long arms, and a feathery fan on the end of my tail.

DILOPHOSAURUS
dy-LOAF-oh-SAW-russ *(HOW YOU PRONOUNCE MY NAME)*

MY FAVORITE FOOD Meat
HOW MUCH I WEIGH 1,000 pounds
HOW BIG I AM Twenty feet in length
HOW BIG I AM COMPARED TO YOU As long as two tigers
REGION I LIVED IN The US
ABOUT ME
I have a long neck and two head crests. My body shape is quite similar to Cryolophosaurus, but without the feathers. I have a small notch in my upper jaw which helps me catch small dinosaurs, such as Scutellosaurus. My sharp claws help with that as well.

EODROMAEUS
ee-o-dro-MAY-uss *(HOW YOU PRONOUNCE MY NAME)*

MY FAVORITE FOOD Small reptiles
HOW MUCH I WEIGH Eleven pounds
HOW BIG I AM Three feet in length
HOW BIG I AM COMPARED TO YOU As big as a raccoon
REGION I LIVED IN South America
ABOUT ME
I'm one of the earliest dinosaurs. Small, light, and nimble, I run across the deserts and plains of South America catching small lizards to eat. My arms and hands are fairly large, with sharp claws that stop my prey from escaping.

HERRERASAURUS
heh-RARE-ah-SAW-russ *(HOW YOU PRONOUNCE MY NAME)*

MY FAVORITE FOOD Meat
HOW MUCH I WEIGH 600 pounds
HOW BIG I AM Twenty feet in length
HOW BIG I AM COMPARED TO YOU As long as two tigers
REGION I LIVED IN Argentina
ABOUT ME
I'm a very early dinosaur and an efficient hunter. I have long arms and three long, clawed fingers on each hand. My legs are powerful and fast, and my teeth are backwards-facing, which keeps prey from escaping.

THEROPOD DINOSAURS

WORD SCRAMBLE

Unscramble these theropod-related words and fill in the boxes

1. ADPTEROR
2. VNICEROAR
3. ERDOOPHT
4. SOALAURLUS
5. UOSNARSYNURTA

ANSWERS: 1. Predator 2. Carnivore 3. Theropod 4. Allosaurus 5. Tyrannosaurus

DID YOU KNOW?
The diet of the Majungasaurus consisted mainly of sauropods.

JURAVENATOR
jaw-ruh-VEN-ah-TOR
HOW YOU PRONOUNCE MY NAME

MY FAVORITE FOOD Small animals and insects

HOW MUCH I WEIGH One pound

HOW BIG I AM Two feet in length

HOW BIG I AM COMPARED TO YOU As big as a chicken

REGION I LIVED IN Germany

ABOUT ME
I wade through the swamps and lagoons of Jurassic Germany at night, hunting for my prey. I'm very small, but that helps me hide from predators. I use my long fingers to grab prey and my serrated teeth to eat it.

MAJUNGASAURUS
mah-JUNG-ah-SAW-russ
HOW YOU PRONOUNCE MY NAME

MY FAVORITE FOOD Meat

HOW MUCH I WEIGH One ton

HOW BIG I AM Twenty feet in length

HOW BIG I AM COMPARED TO YOU An adult human would just about reach up to my shoulders

REGION I LIVED IN Madagascar

ABOUT ME
I'm the top predator on the flood plains of Madagascar. My tiny arms are pretty useless during a hunt, but my serrated teeth are more than enough for me to attack and defeat my prey. I also eat other dinosaurs – including smaller Majungasaurus.

WATCH THIS!
THE WATERY TALE OF SPINOSAURUS

SCAN WITH YOUR PHONE OR TABLET
https://bit.ly/3uXTj6e

HOW BIG IS THE PACK?

Some theropods, such as Mapusaurus, hunted in packs. How many Mapusaurus can you spot on this page?

MASIAKASAURUS
mah-SHEE-ah-kah-SAW-russ *(HOW YOU PRONOUNCE MY NAME)*

- **MY FAVORITE FOOD** — Fish and small animals
- **HOW MUCH I WEIGH** — Seventy-seven pounds
- **HOW BIG I AM** — Seven feet in length
- **HOW BIG I AM COMPARED TO YOU** — As big as a goat
- **REGION I LIVED IN** — Madagascar
- **ABOUT ME** — My tail makes up half the length of my body, but that's not my most unusual feature – it's my teeth! They scheckmark out away from my face. Teeth like this are no good at tearing meat, but that's okay because I hunt for fish and smaller animals and swallow them whole.

MAPUSAURUS
mah-puh-SAW-russ *(HOW YOU PRONOUNCE MY NAME)*

- **MY FAVORITE FOOD** — Meat
- **HOW MUCH I WEIGH** — Three tons
- **HOW BIG I AM** — Thirty-six feet in length
- **HOW BIG I AM COMPARED TO YOU** — As long as a truck
- **REGION I LIVED IN** — Argentina
- **ABOUT ME** — I'm another big theropod and another fierce hunter, just like my cousin Giganotosaurus. I'm intelligent for a dinosaur, too. Sometimes I hunt in packs with other Mapusaurus. Working together helps us defeat larger prey, such as other sauropods.

MEGALOSAURUS
meh-GUH-luh-SAW-russ *(HOW YOU PRONOUNCE MY NAME)*

- **MY FAVORITE FOOD** — Meat
- **HOW MUCH I WEIGH** — Two tons
- **HOW BIG I AM** — Thirty feet in length
- **HOW BIG I AM COMPARED TO YOU** — As long as a double-decker bus
- **REGION I LIVED IN** — The UK
- **ABOUT ME** — I hunt and eat all day long in the prehistoric woodlands of the UK. My muscular thighs are built for speed, and my tail helps me balance while I chase my prey. I have long claws on my hands which I use to catch my prey, and deadly teeth for when I go in for the kill.

OVIRAPTOR
Oh-vee-RAP-tor *(HOW YOU PRONOUNCE MY NAME)*

- **MY FAVORITE FOOD** — Meat, plants, and fruit
- **HOW MUCH I WEIGH** — Forty-four pounds
- **HOW BIG I AM** — Seven feet in length
- **HOW BIG I AM COMPARED TO YOU** — The size of a sheep
- **REGION I LIVED IN** — Mongolia
- **ABOUT ME** — I'm one of the later theropods, from the end of the Cretaceous period. I have a head crest and a horny beak. My beak is toothless but strong enough to break open nuts and seeds. I also eat small animals, including little lizards.

THEROPOD DINOSAURS

SINOSAUROPTERYX
SY-nah-SAW-op-ter-ix *(HOW YOU PRONOUNCE MY NAME)*

MY FAVORITE FOOD — Meat
HOW MUCH I WEIGH — One pound
HOW BIG I AM — Three feet in length
HOW BIG I AM COMPARED TO YOU — A bit longer than a fox
REGION I LIVED IN — China
ABOUT ME — I'm small and light – perfect for running quietly through the forests. I was the first dinosaur to be discovered to have feathers. Scientists couldn't believe it! My fuzzy feathers kept me warm while I hunted for small insects and rodents.

SPINOSAURUS
SPY-noh-SAW-russ *(HOW YOU PRONOUNCE MY NAME)*

MY FAVORITE FOOD — Fish
HOW MUCH I WEIGH — Eleven tons
HOW BIG I AM — Fifty feet in length
HOW BIG I AM COMPARED TO YOU — As long as a humpback whale
REGION I LIVED IN — Egypt and Morocco
ABOUT ME — I live beside rivers and lakes, which is perfect because my favorite food is fish. The three long claws on my hands help me swipe fish from the water, and I use my cone-shaped teeth and long jaws to trap and eat them. I have a back sail to attract a mate and a paddle-like tail for moving about in water.

THERIZINOSAURUS
THERRY-zin-oh-SAW-russ *(HOW YOU PRONOUNCE MY NAME)*

MY FAVORITE FOOD — Plants
HOW MUCH I WEIGH — Five tons
HOW BIG I AM — Thirty-three feet in length
HOW BIG I AM COMPARED TO YOU — I'm as big as a truck
REGION I LIVED IN — Mongolia
ABOUT ME — I'm a herbivorous theropod. Even though I have huge claws, I don't eat meat. I can reach quite high to eat leaves from the trees and I use my big claws to pull branches down to my mouth. My claws are also a pretty good defense against predators.

TYRANNOSAURUS
TY-ran-oh-SAW-russ *(HOW YOU PRONOUNCE MY NAME)*

MY FAVORITE FOOD — Meat
HOW MUCH I WEIGH — Eight tons
HOW BIG I AM — Forty-three feet
HOW BIG I AM COMPARED TO YOU — I'm bigger than a helicopter
REGION I LIVED IN — Canada and the US
ABOUT ME — I'm sure you've heard of me – I'm probably the most famous dinosaur of all time. I'm huge and heavy, fast and fearless. My eyesight and sense of smell are excellent, and my jaws are so powerful they can bite through bone and eat a dinosaur the size of a pig!

THEROPOD DINOSAURS

The word theropod means "beast foot." But that's not very descriptive. Even among theropods, feet – and pretty much everything else – varied. In fact, theropods are the most diverse of all the dinosaur groups. They had some truly amazing features, from feathery elbows and unusual head crests to killing claws, back sails, and scheckmark-out teeth!

DID YOU KNOW?
Giganotosaurus was fast enough to win a 330-foot sprint

WINGS
Some small, feathery dinosaurs were actually capable of flight. They were the ancestors of modern birds. Other dinosaurs had feathery features, like elbow feathers, even though they couldn't fly.

OSTRICH-LIKE OMNIVORES
Some dinosaurs, known as ornithomimosaurs, had ostrich-like features, including a beak, feathers, and the ability to run fast.

KILLER CLAWS
Dromaeosaurids, also sometimes called raptors, were small, feathered predators with an extra large, curved foot claw that was held in a raised position while walking to keep it sharp.

HERBIVORES WITH AWESOME HAND CLAWS
Therizinosaurus were feathery herbivores with unusually long hand claws.

THE BIG ONES
Big heads, sharp teeth, and small hands – we all know what these terrifying predators looked like. There were many different subgroups of these predators, including the allosaurids with their long, narrow skulls and three-fingered hands and tyrannosaurs with their larger skulls and two-fingered hands.

WATCH THIS!
AN ORNITHOMIMOSAUR MYSTERY

SCAN WITH YOUR PHONE OR TABLET
https://bit.ly/3OduyMa

ACROCANTHOSAURUS
ak-ro-KAN-tho-SAW-russ *(HOW YOU PRONOUNCE MY NAME)*

- **MY FAVORITE FOOD** — Meat
- **HOW MUCH I WEIGH** — Seven tons
- **HOW BIG I AM** — Thirty-eight feet in length
- **HOW BIG I AM COMPARED TO YOU** — I'm longer than two crocodiles
- **REGION I LIVED IN** — Canada and the US
- **ABOUT ME** — I'm one of the largest theropods – even the smaller theropods are scared of me! I use my sharp jaws to catch my prey and then my claws to kill it. I have spines all the way down my back and tail that scientists think might have supported a sail or a hump.

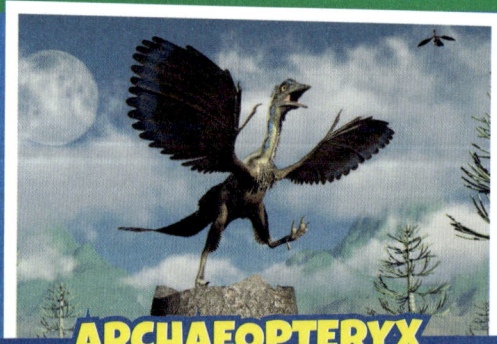

ARCHAEOPTERYX
ar-kee-OP-ter-ix *(HOW YOU PRONOUNCE MY NAME)*

- **MY FAVORITE FOOD** — Meat
- **HOW MUCH I WEIGH** — Two pounds
- **HOW BIG I AM** — Two feet in length
- **HOW BIG I AM COMPARED TO YOU** — I'm the size of a crow
- **REGION I LIVED IN** — Germany
- **ABOUT ME** — I have feathers and wings, and I can even fly short distances – but I'm not a bird. I'm still a dinosaur. See my pointy teeth and clawed hands and feet? My tail is covered in feathers, but it's bony underneath. I am one of the oldest flying dinosaurs.

THEROPOD DINOSAURS

AUCASAURUS
AW-ka-SAW-russ
(HOW YOU PRONOUNCE MY NAME)

MY FAVORITE FOOD Meat
HOW MUCH I WEIGH One ton
HOW BIG I AM Twenty feet in length
HOW BIG I AM COMPARED TO YOU
I'm the size of a great white shark
REGION I LIVED IN Argentina
ABOUT ME
I'm smaller than most large theropods and my arms are very small, with tiny claws, but that doesn't stop me. I hunt across the plains of South America searching for prey, including dinosaurs that are smaller than me. My stiff, outstretched tail helps me balance when chasing my next meal.

BARYONYX
bah-ree-ON-ix
(HOW YOU PRONOUNCE MY NAME)

MY FAVORITE FOOD Meat
HOW MUCH I WEIGH Two tons
HOW BIG I AM Thirty-three feet in length
HOW BIG I AM COMPARED TO YOU
Twice as long as a saltwater crocodile, with thumb claws as long as cucumbers
REGION I LIVED IN Spain and the UK
ABOUT ME
My crocodile-like head has powerful jaws and lots of small sharp teeth, which I use to eat fish from rivers and lakes. My big thumb claws help me catch the slippery fish. I can also hunt for larger prey on land when I want to.

CARCHARODONTOSAURUS
KAR-ka-ro-DON-to-SAW-russ
(HOW YOU PRONOUNCE MY NAME)

MY FAVORITE FOOD Meat
HOW MUCH I WEIGH Eight tons
HOW BIG I AM Forty-three feet in length
HOW BIG I AM COMPARED TO YOU
Bigger than two great white sharks
REGION I LIVED IN North Africa
ABOUT ME
My name means "teeth like a great white shark." But I'm twice the size of a great white shark, and way scarier. My jaws are as long as a twelve year old and I can swallow small dinosaurs whole. Nearby animals, beware.

CITIPATI
sih-tee-PAH-tee
(HOW YOU PRONOUNCE MY NAME)

MY FAVORITE FOOD Leaves, seeds, and small animals
HOW MUCH I WEIGH 200 pounds
HOW BIG I AM Ten feet in length
HOW BIG I AM COMPARED TO YOU
Slightly bigger than a tiger
REGION I LIVED IN Mongolia
ABOUT ME
I'm another birdlike dinosaur. I have a toothless beak, feathers on my body, and small, wing-like features on my arms. But I can't fly. I run on my strong legs, hunting for small animals and foraging for seeds in the forests before going back to my nest to sit on my eggs.

CONFUCIUSORNIS
kon-few-shus-OR-niss *(HOW YOU PRONOUNCE MY NAME)*

- **MY FAVORITE FOOD** — Plants and small fish
- **HOW MUCH I WEIGH** — Two pounds
- **HOW BIG I AM** — Two feet in length
- **HOW BIG I AM COMPARED TO YOU** — I'm the size of a crow
- **REGION I LIVED IN** — China
- **ABOUT ME** — I look like a bird with my large wings, toothless beak, and long feathery tail. But if you look closely you'll see I still have claws on my wings. I can fly, but not for extended periods of time. Like my older cousin Archaeopteryx, I am an ancient ancestor of modern birds.

CRYOLOPHOSAURUS
cry-o-LOAF-o-SAW-russ *(HOW YOU PRONOUNCE MY NAME)*

- **MY FAVORITE FOOD** — Meat
- **HOW MUCH I WEIGH** — 1,100 pounds
- **HOW BIG I AM** — Twenty-six feet in length
- **HOW BIG I AM COMPARED TO YOU** — As long as four dolphins
- **REGION I LIVED IN** — Antarctica
- **ABOUT ME** — I hunt in the forests of Antarctica and my feathers keep me warm. I am one of the largest theropods of the early Jurassic period, and my nice bony head crest makes me even taller! I use my long arms to grab prey and my sharp teeth to cut through flesh.

DEINONYCHUS
dy-NON-ih-kuss *(HOW YOU PRONOUNCE MY NAME)*

- **MY FAVORITE FOOD** — Meat
- **HOW MUCH I WEIGH** — 220 pounds
- **HOW BIG I AM** — Four yards in length
- **HOW BIG I AM COMPARED TO YOU** — I'm as long as a rhino
- **REGION I LIVED IN** — The US
- **ABOUT ME** — I'm a deadly hunter. Fast and intelligent, I track my prey. I work in a pack with other Deinonychus to attack much larger dinosaurs. My arms are quite long for a theropod, and I use them to slash at my prey. I have killing claws on my feet – they are enormous!

EORAPTOR
ee-o-RAP-ter *(HOW YOU PRONOUNCE MY NAME)*

- **MY FAVORITE FOOD** — Meat
- **HOW MUCH I WEIGH** — Twenty-two pounds
- **HOW BIG I AM** — Three feet in length
- **HOW BIG I AM COMPARED TO YOU** — About the size of a cat
- **REGION I LIVED IN** — Argentina
- **ABOUT ME** — I'm small and light, which makes me a good runner. I catch my prey with my hands, and I use my claws and teeth to rip and eat it. I live in the same environment as many other early theropods, including Herrerasaurus.

THEROPOD DINOSAURS

GIGANOTOSAURUS
jig-AN-ot-o-SAW-russ

HOW YOU PRONOUNCE MY NAME

MY FAVORITE FOOD Meat

HOW MUCH I WEIGH Nine tons

HOW BIG I AM Forty feet in length

HOW BIG I AM COMPARED TO YOU
Three ten-year-olds standing one on top of the other would reach my hip!

REGION I LIVED IN Argentina

ABOUT ME
I'm big and I'm fast. If that doesn't scare you enough, just take a look at my teeth. They are thin and sharp, like lots of little saws. I am top of the food chain in Argentina and I am mighty enough to hunt large prey. Even a sauropod like Argentinosaurus can't stop me when I'm hungry.

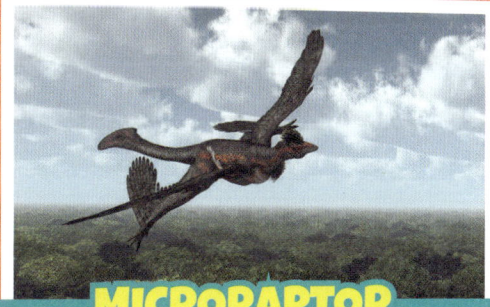

MICRORAPTOR
MY-crow-RAP-tor

HOW YOU PRONOUNCE MY NAME

MY FAVORITE FOOD Small animals, such as lizards

HOW MUCH I WEIGH Two pounds

HOW BIG I AM Two-and-a-half feet in length

HOW BIG I AM COMPARED TO YOU
I'm the size of a chicken

REGION I LIVED IN China

ABOUT ME
I love my shiny black feathers and four wings. I use them to glide from tree to tree, but I can't fly for long distances. I have small, sharp teeth in my beak that help me catch fish.

CRACK THE CODE!

Decipher the secret message to learn an awesome theropod fact.

EXAMPLE:
THEROPODS RULE

HERE'S A SECRET MESSAGE. CAN YOU DECIPHER IT?

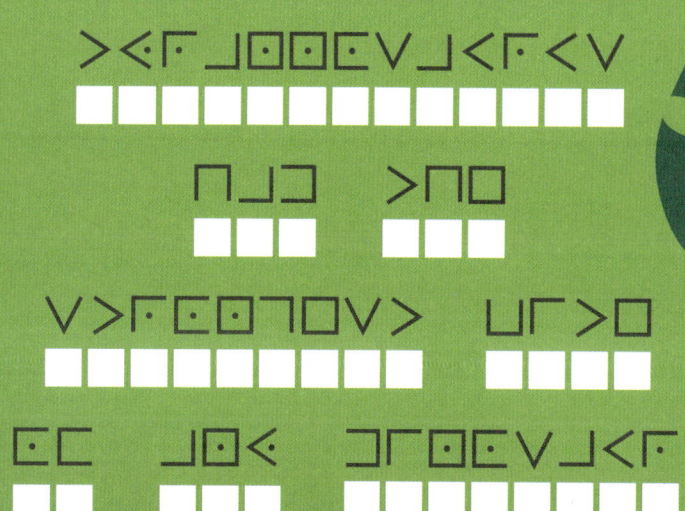

ANSWER: Tyrannosaurus had the strongest bite of any dinosaur

THEROPODS BY NUMBERS

Fill in the missing numbers to complete these theropod facts

DEINOCHEIRUS HAS  **TAIL FANS**

TYRANNOTITAN HAS  **TEETH**

DILOPHOSAURUS HAS  **HEAD CRESTS**

SPINOSAURUS HAS  **CLAWS ON EACH HAND**

ANSWERS: 2, 60, 1, 3

MATCH IT UP

Match these dinosaurs to their feature

1 TYRANNOSAURUS

2 SPINOSAURUS

3 DEINOCHEIRUS

4 CRYOLOPHOSAURUS

5 ACROCANTHOSAURUS

A BACK SAIL

B COVERED IN FEATHERS

C LOOKS LIKE AN OSTRICH

D HUMPED BACK

E EXCELLENT EYESIGHT AND SENSE OF SMELL

ANSWERS: 1E, 2A, 3C, 4B, 5D

NEOVENATOR
nee-o-VEN-ah-tor — HOW YOU PRONOUNCE MY NAME

MY FAVORITE FOOD Meat
HOW MUCH I WEIGH One ton
HOW BIG I AM Twenty-five feet in length
HOW BIG I AM COMPARED TO YOU
Longer than an African elephant
REGION I LIVED IN The UK
ABOUT ME
I have three very long claws on my hands, which help me attack my prey. I chase Iguanodon and other herbivores across the woodlands of ancient England. After slashing with my claws, I use my blade-like teeth to kill prey.

TRUE OR FALSE?

ALL THEROPODS ARE MEAT-EATERS
TRUE ☐ OR FALSE ☐

ALL THEROPODS HAD TWO CLAWS ON EACH HAND
TRUE ☐ OR FALSE ☐

MOST THEROPODS HAD SERRATED TEETH
TRUE ☐ OR FALSE ☐

SOME THEROPOD WERE COVERED IN FEATHERS
TRUE ☐ OR FALSE ☐

THERE WERE NO FLYING THEROPODS
TRUE ☐ OR FALSE ☐

BIRDS ARE THEROPODS
TRUE ☐ OR FALSE ☐

ANSWERS: False, False, True, True, False, True

PELECANIMIMUS
peh-lih-kan-ih-MY-muss — HOW YOU PRONOUNCE MY NAME

MY FAVORITE FOOD Meat
HOW MUCH I WEIGH Sixty-six pounds
HOW BIG I AM Eight feet in length
HOW BIG I AM COMPARED TO YOU
I'm as big as a horse
REGION I LIVED IN Spain
ABOUT ME
I'm the same kind of dinosaur as Deinocheirus – we both look like ostriches – just smaller. I have feathers and really long legs and feet, but I'm most proud of my teeth. I have about 220. That's more than any other theropod.

THEROPOD DINOSAURS

STRUTHIOMIMUS
STROO-thee-oh-MY-muss *(HOW YOU PRONOUNCE MY NAME)*

- **MY FAVORITE FOOD** Leaves and meat
- **HOW MUCH I WEIGH** 900 pounds
- **HOW BIG I AM** Eighteen feet in length
- **HOW BIG I AM COMPARED TO YOU** Almost twice the size of an ostrich
- **REGION I LIVED IN** Canada
- **ABOUT ME** My name means "ostrich mimic" – it's true, I do look like an ostrich. I even run at about the same speed. I have long claws on my hands and feet and a long, feathered tail. My long neck helps me reach food high in the trees.

DID YOU KNOW?
Deinonychus means "terrible claw." I think we all know which claw that refers to!

TROODON
TROO-oh-don *(HOW YOU PRONOUNCE MY NAME)*

- **MY FAVORITE FOOD** Whatever meat I can find
- **HOW MUCH I WEIGH** 110 pounds
- **HOW BIG I AM** Six feet in length
- **HOW BIG I AM COMPARED TO YOU** I'm a bit larger than a wolf
- **REGION I LIVED IN** The US
- **ABOUT ME** I'm pretty intelligent for a dinosaur. I have good eyesight and sharp, serrated teeth. I look a bit like a bird because I'm covered with feathers, but I can't fly. I was one of the first dinosaurs to be discovered, but for a long time scientists thought I was a lizard.

TYRANNOTITAN
TY-ran-o-TY-tan *(HOW YOU PRONOUNCE MY NAME)*

- **MY FAVORITE FOOD** Meat
- **HOW MUCH I WEIGH** Six tons
- **HOW BIG I AM** Forty feet in length
- **HOW BIG I AM COMPARED TO YOU** I'm as long as three cars
- **REGION I LIVED IN** Argentina
- **ABOUT ME** I'm big, strong, and hungry. I have sixty teeth covered in sharp little bumps called denticles. They help me devour my prey. I need to eat a lot to fuel my huge, powerful body. You might think I'm a close relative of Tyrannosaurus, but I'm more closely related to Giganotosaurus.

VELOCIRAPTOR
vell-oss-ih-RAP-tor *(HOW YOU PRONOUNCE MY NAME)*

- **MY FAVORITE FOOD** Meat
- **HOW MUCH I WEIGH** Thirty-three pounds
- **HOW BIG I AM** Seven feet in length
- **HOW BIG I AM COMPARED TO YOU** I'm the size of a goat
- **REGION I LIVED IN** Mongolia
- **ABOUT ME** I'm a deadly predator. I'm fast, feathered, fierce, and go straight for the kill. I use my huge, curved foot claws to slash at my prey. Then I hold them down with the long claws on my hands while I tear at them with my teeth.

DID YOU KNOW?
There's ongoing debate among scientists about whether Eoraptor is a theropod or a sauropod.

RECORD-BREAKING DINOSAURS

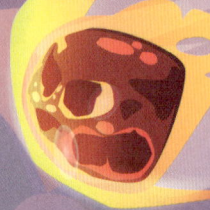

Dinosaurs were incredible creatures. They roamed the Earth for hundreds of millions of years, evolving and flourishing. They developed features that made them the best at what they needed to do – from hunting, digesting plants, fishing, finding a mate, self-defense and chewing. It's no wonder dinosaurs hold so many world records. Let's find out about some of the all-time record-breaking dinosaurs.

LONGEST HORNS
TRICERATOPS, COAHUILACERATOPS, AND TOROSAURUS
Four feet long – as tall as an eight year old

LARGEST
ARGENTINOSAURUS
115 feet long – half as long as a jumbo jet

LARGEST SKULL
PENTACERATOPS
Nine feet – the size of an ostrich

STRONGEST BITE
OF ANY LAND ANIMAL
TYRANNOSAURUS
Six tons of pressure – enough to crush a car

LONGEST CLAWS
THERIZINOSAURUS
Two feet long – as big as a one-year-old child

FASTEST
ORNITHOMIMUS
Sixty miles per hour

MOST HORNS
KOSMOCERATOPS
Fifteen horns on its huge head

LONGEST CARNIVOROUS DINOSAUR
SPINOSAURUS
Fifty feet long – as long as a humpback whale

MOST TEETH
EDMONTOSAURUS
Its dental battery held 1,500 teeth

LONGEST CREST
PARASAUROLOPHUS
Three feet long – as long as a baseball bat

THICKEST SKULL
PACHYCEPHALOSAURUS
One foot thick – forty times thicker than a human skull

FIRST FOSSILS
MEGALOSAURUS
The first dinosaur fossils were discovered in 1824. They were later identified as Megalosaurus bones

RECORD-BREAKING DINOSAURS

LONGEST ARMS
OF A TWO-LEGGED DINOSAUR
DEINOCHEIRUS
Eight feet long – that's two eight-year-old children standing one on top of the other

MOST TEETH
OF A CARNIVOROUS DINOSAUR
PELECANIMIMUS
220 teeth

ASTONISHING
Dinosaurs dominated our planet for much longer than humans have even been alive. Despite this – and despite the fact that some dinosaurs were so enormous – we didn't know they existed at all until 1842. That's less than 200 years ago. In 1842, a British scientist named Richard Owens first used the word "Dinosauria," which means "terrible lizard" in Greek. He coined the word to explain the huge fossils that had been discovered in England over the previous twenty years or so. The fossils looked reptilian, but much bigger.

FIRST FEATHERS
FIRST NON-FLYING DINOSAUR TO BE DISCOVERED WITH FEATHERS
SINOSAUROPTERYX
Discovered in 1996, Sinosauropteryx surprised everyone by showing that it wasn't only the flying dinosaurs that had feathers

LONGEST DINOSAUR NAME
MICROPACHYCEPHALOSAURUS
23 letters long

LONGEST NECK
SAUROPOSEIDON
Forty feet long – as long as three basketball hoops

WORD SCRAMBLE
Unscramble the letters to discover five dinosaur record breakers

1. eocmraotokpss
2. eoonutsmardus
3. aosealurmusg
4. tapcraetoepsn
5. usaahuroplropsa

ANSWERS: 1. Kosmoceratops 2. Edmontosaurus 3. Megalosaurus 4. Pentaceratops 5. Parasaurolophus

81

END OF CHAPTER: PUZZLES & ACTIVITIES

LET'S PUT YOUR THEROPOD KNOWLEDGE TO THE TEST WITH THESE PUZZLES AND ACTIVITIES

QUIZ

WHAT HAVE YOU LEARNED?

WHICH OF THESE IS A HERBIVORE?
A. Archaeopteryx
B. Therizinosaurus
C. Spinosaurus

WHAT WAS ONE OF THE FIRST-EVER THEROPODS?
A: Eodromaeus
B: Velociraptor
C: Giganotosaurus

WHICH PREDATOR HAD SPIKES UNDER ITS CHIN?
A: Carnotaurus
B: Deinonychus
C: Megalosaurus

WHAT WAS THE FIRST DINOSAUR TO BE DISCOVERED TO HAVE FEATHERS?
A: Velociraptor
B: Cryolophosaurus
C: Sinosauropteryx

WHICH DINOSAUR HAS TWO HEAD CRESTS?
A: Majungasaurus
B: Dilophosaurus
C: Compsognathus

ANSWERS: B, A, A, C, B

HELP THE HUNTER FIND ITS PREY

DILOPHOSAURUS — **ARCHAEOPTERYX** — **SPINOSAURUS**
MICRORAPTOR — **TYRANNOSAURUS** — **ALLOSAURUS**

MAYFLY — Archaeopteryx was able to catch slow-flying insects.

PREHISTORIC LIZARD — A Microraptor fossil was found with a small lizard in its stomach.

ANKYLOSAURUS — Ankylosaurus would have been on the menu for Tyrannosaurus.

SCUTELLOSAURUS — Small dinosaurs such as Scutellosaurus would have been easy prey.

MAWSONIA — Big fish like Mawsonia would be no problem for Spinosaurus.

STEGOSAURUS — A fierce battle would take place between these two.

END OF CHAPTER: PUZZLES & ACTIVITIES

FILL IN THE BLANKS

1. Theropods walked the Earth from the Late _____ period until the end of the _____ period.
2. Theropods walk on _____ legs.
3. Most theropods are _____, but there are a few _____ as well.
4. Many theropods had _____.
5. Theropods are the ancestors of modern-day _____.

TRIASSIC | SIX | HORNS | SHEEP | TWO | CARNIVORES | FOUR | JURASSIC | SAUROPODS | CRETACEOUS | HERBIVORES | FEATHERS | BIRDS | HEAD FRILLS | CERATOPSIANS | KANGAROOS

ANSWER: 1. Triassic, Cretaceous 2. Two 3. Carnivores, Herbivores 4. Feathers 5. Birds

COLOR ME!

ROARSOME VIDEOS

WHAT IS A THEROPOD?
https://bit.ly/3O1jS3d

INSIDE AN OVIRAPTOR EGG
https://bit.ly/37zyK8c

WHY DID TYRANNOSAURUS HAVE SUCH SMALL ARMS?
https://bit.ly/3raY2QU

WHAT IS THE COOLEST DINOSAUR? ASK THE EXPERTS
https://bit.ly/3LQRdM9

SCAN WITH YOUR PHONE OR TABLET

WHAT DO YOU THINK?

Some dinosaurs grew to be enormous. Tyrannosaurus was Forty-three feet long, which is longer than a helicopter. What other objects can you think of that are around the same size as the mighty Tyrannosaurus?

SCAN HERE!
LEARN HOW TO DRAW A TYRANNOSAURUS

SCAN WITH YOUR PHONE OR TABLET
https://bit.ly/3O0IJVY

DIY DINO BOX HAT

Recycle an old cardboard box into a 3D dinosaur hat

WHAT YOU'LL NEED
- Pencil
- Cardboard box
- Scissors
- Tape
- Markers
- Other arts and crafts materials (optional)

INSTRUCTIONS

1. Use a pencil to plan the different features you are going to add to your box hat.
2. There are many dinosaur features you could add to your hat. How about horns, crests, feathers, ridges, spikes, osteoderms, frills, or a beak? Think about the shape of the teeth: will you go for pointy, conical, serrated, or backwards-curving?
3. With scissors, carefully cut out the base of the box – where your head will go – and other features you want to cut out, such as the mouth and sharp teeth. Ask an adult to help you if needed.
4. With the pieces of cardboard you've cut away, create external features, such as eye ridges, spikes, or horns. Use tape to add these to your hat.
5. Use markers or extra arts and crafts materials to complete your hat. Will you make the eyes a scary yellow color? Will you add a scaly pattern to your dinosaur skin? Will you add some battle scars?

WORD SEARCH

How many large theropod dinosaurs can you find in this word search?

```
R A D E I N O C H E I R U S R I
E A S C H B Y U I O M S A P D T
B U E N E O V E N A T O R I T Y
I C A R T S A B K A D M L N P R
M A P U S A U R U S B R G O N A
R S E F G H B A V B N H Y S I N
K A L L O S A U R U S E R A L N
B U T Y H S R E T H A U R U B O
G R H K M K Y L O U Y A F R E S
R U B N M K O A S A U R B U N A
E S F G A B N R G T Y J K S Q U
L P O K M D Y T J A D R Y N B R
S A U R E R X A V G N H A U R U
E R D I L O P H O S A U R U S S
A L B E R T O S A U R U S F T Q
```

- ALBERTOSAURUS
- ALLOSAURUS
- AUCASAURUS
- BARYONYX
- DEINOCHEIRUS
- DILOPHOSAURUS
- MAPUSAURUS
- NEOVENATOR
- SPINOSAURUS
- TYRANNOSAURUS

WHO AM I?

Use the clues to work out which theropod this is

I'M A CARNIVORE
I'M TWENTY FEET LONG
I HAVE TINY ARMS
I LIVED IN ARGENTINA
I WEIGH ONE TON

ANSWER: Aucasaurus

END OF CHAPTER: PUZZLES & ACTIVITIES

DOT TO DOT

Complete this illustration of Herrerasaurus, one of the first-ever theropods

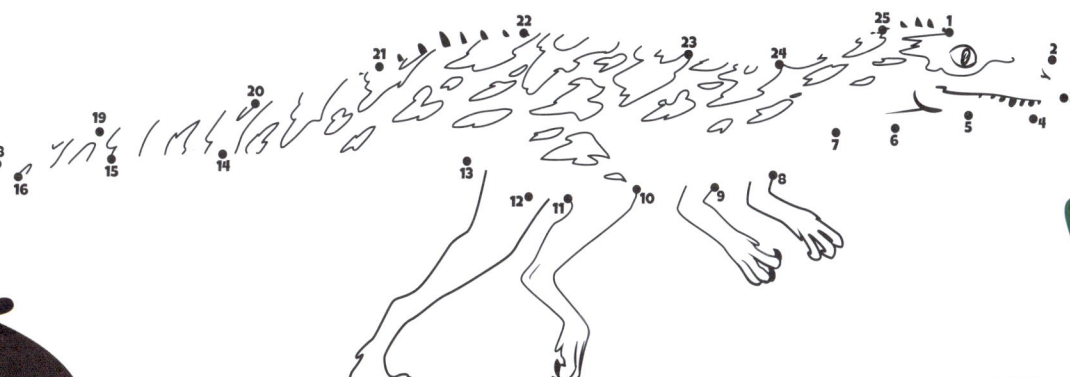

SCAN HERE!
WHY DINOSAUR POOP IS USEFUL
SCAN WITH YOUR PHONE OR TABLET
https://bit.ly/3KvQ7Fy

CROSSWORD

Fit the words into the crossword and unscramble the letters in the yellow squares to find the name of a big theropod

- VELOCIRAPTOR
- AUCASAURUS
- ALLOSAURUS
- PREDATOR
- OVIRAPTOR
- TEETH
- CREST
- BIRD
- BITE
- FISH
- PREY
- EORAPTOR
- SERRATED
- TROODON

THE SECRET WORD IS _____

ANSWERS: Dilophosaurus

DIY FOSSILS

Make your own dinosaur fossils by pressing templates onto clay or salt dough. Use the fossil prints for decoration or to create your own dinosaur fossil hunt

WHAT YOU'LL NEED
- Thick card or foam paper
- Pencil
- Scissors
- Clay or salt dough

SALT DOUGH RECIPE
- Two cups of plain flour
- Five tablespoons of salt
- Half a cup of water
- Food coloring (optional)

Mix the flour and salt together, then add the water and mix until it becomes a ball of dough. Add food coloring if you want your fossil finds to be a different color.

INSTRUCTIONS

1. Draw the outlines of dinosaur bones on your card or foam paper. You only need one of each type of bone, as you can use the template as much as needed to make your fossils. Take your time and redo them until you are happy with the shapes.
2. Carefully cut around your dinosaur bone shapes until you have a collection of templates.
3. Roll out your clay or dough so it's about one inch thick.
4. Press your bone templates firmly into the clay or dough so they form a strong impression. But don't press all the way down.
5. Use each of your templates as often as necessary until you've created a fossil pattern or skeleton that you're happy with.
6. Leave your clay to dry or bake your salt dough. Place it on a baking tray lined with parchment paper and heat it in your oven on its lowest setting for at least three hours. Get an adult to help with the oven.

TRY THIS!
Think about dinosaur fossils. Most finds don't include perfect skeletons. Think about how you can create realistic-looking fossils.
- What positions have dinosaur skeletons been found in?
- If a dinosaur skeleton is incomplete, why might this be?
- Some dinosaurs have been found locked in battle. How could you recreate this?

SAFETY FIRST! Ask an adult to help if you're using the oven

BATTLE UP

These dinosaurs probably battled against each other millions of years ago. Discuss with your friends who would win, and why

ALLOSAURUS VS STEGOSAURUS
ARCHAEOPTERYX VS COMPSOGNATHUS
TYRANNOSAURUS VS ANKYLOSAURUS

GET CREATIVE!

Write your own short story about a dinosaur. Use this space to plan your story out

Think of your main character – is it a dinosaur or a human who finds a dinosaur? If it's a dinosaur, is it a scary one or a nice one?

Think about what type of story you want to write. It could be short and simple, like a fairy tale, or it could be a terrifying adventure. Maybe you want to write about a dinosaur's journey across the prehistoric world? What story will you come up with?

Think about your storyline. What will happen and what will your main character learn by the end of the story?

END OF CHAPTER: **PUZZLES & ACTIVITIES**

BIG AND SMALL

Follow the correct path through the maze to put these predators in size order from smallest to largest

MICRORAPTOR
TROODON
CITIPATI
SPINOSAURUS
TYRANNOSAURUS
AUCASAURUS
MEGALOSAURUS

DESIGN A DEINOCHEIRUS

They're known for looking rather unusual – funny feathers, a back hump, tail fan, and extremely long arms. Color in this Deinocheirus. How unusual will you make it look?

DINOSAURS IN THE MOVIES

JURASSIC PARK (1993)
https://bit.ly/3Jsw1KF

THE GOOD DINOSAUR (2015)
https://bit.ly/3JjAmzT

THE LAND BEFORE TIME (1988)
https://bit.ly/3JmYeTk

ICE AGE: DAWN OF THE DINOSAURS (2009)
https://bit.ly/3rbppKH

SCAN WITH YOUR PHONE OR TABLET

WHICH THEROPOD ARE YOU?

1. WHAT DO YOU LIKE TO MUNCH ON?
A. Small animals and insects
B. Plants
C. Meat
D. Fish

2. HOW WOULD YOU LIKE TO GET AROUND?
A. Flying
B. Walking
C. Stomping
D. Paddling

3. DIFFERENT GROUPS OF THEROPODS COULD LOOK COMPLETELY DIFFERENT TO EACH OTHER. WHICH OF THESE FEATURES DO YOU WISH YOU HAD?
A. Wings
B. Super long claws
C. Enormous teeth
D. A back sail

4. HOW DO YOU LIKE TO EAT YOUR DINNER?
A. After a ferocious battle
B. During a relaxing day spent grazing
C. Hunt it down and swallow it whole
D. After a fishing trip

MOSTLY A: YOU'RE AN ARCHAEOPTERYX
Small but fierce, the Archaeopteryx hunted its prey and attacked it with its sharp claws and pointy teeth. It could fly from tree to tree using its feathery wings.

MOSTLY B: YOU'RE A THERIZINOSAURUS
Therizinosaurus was a rare herbivorous theropod. It used its incredibly long front claws to pull branches down so it could graze on the delicious leaves.

MOSTLY C: YOU'RE A TYRANNOSAURUS
The ferocious Tyrannosaurus stomped across the Cretaceous landscape, terrifying all the creatures in its path. It stalked and hunted its prey before attacking with its claws, teeth, and powerful bite.

MOSTLY D: YOU'RE A SPINOSAURUS
A very large predator, Spinosaurus evolved as an expert fisher. It used its tail and feet to wade through water and its teeth to catch and eat fish.

ODD ONE OUT

Which of these dinosaurs is not an ornithomimosaur?

A   B   C

ANSWER: C

DINOSAUR PROJECT

If you just can't get enough of dinosaurs, why not work on a detailed dinosaur project?

1. Choose your favorite dinosaur.
2. Research your chosen dinosaur using reference books and the internet. Note down:

- What kind of dinosaur it was
- When it lived
- Which other dinosaurs and prehistoric creatures lived at the same time
- Where it lived
- What habitat it lived in
- What its diet was
- Who its predators were
- What it looked like
- What special features it had
- What made this dinosaur special or unique
- Can you find any cool videos about your favorite dinosaur?
- Create your project page by page. Decide on each page's heading, like habitat or diet
- Use your notes to write out the most important facts. Make your pages look nice with borders, doodles, sketches, colors, pictures, or illustrations
- Create a collage of images of your chosen dinosaur
- Draw or paint your dinosaur. You could even label its special features
- Put your project together in a binder or staple your pages into a beautiful book

END OF CHAPTER: PUZZLES & ACTIVITIES

WORD SEARCH

How many small theropod dinosaurs can you find in this word search?

```
V E L D E I N O N Y C H U S W Q
P R A P R O R N L O P A V R B V
E B N C I T I P A T I S F A L E
L S E R A P T F H T A V M P I L
E D P E L I A D E I H K I L P O
C O E L O P H Y S I S V C G B C
A K H E R R E R A S A U R U S I
N T O R A P T H U I K P O A B R
I G R B E O R A P T O R R S T A
M E V G H M A K I R T Y A L E P
I O F R H J P Q B O J K P M P T
M R O V I R A P T O R N T O R O
U A D E I V B A E D H Y O L M R
S P O Q V E L I F O E B R D S A
T L N J U R A V E N A T O R A O
```

- CITIPATI
- EORAPTOR
- JURAVENATOR
- DEINONYCHUS
- COELOPHYSIS
- HERRERASAURUS
- MICRORAPTOR
- PELECANIMIMUS
- OVIRAPTOR
- TROODON
- VELOCIRAPTOR

MAKE A DINOSAUR DIORAMA WITH AN ACTIVE VOLCANO

When dinosaurs roamed the Earth, the planet was very different to how it is now. There were lots of active volcanoes, spewing smoke into the air and pouring lava down their sides whenever they erupted. Create your own dinosaur diorama with the amazing special effects of an active volcano.

WHAT YOU'LL NEED

- A small plastic water bottle
- Pieces of cardstock or newspaper, flour and water for papier-mâché
- Scissors
- Tape
- Paint
- Measuring jug
- One tablespoon soap
- One tablespoon baking soda
- Two tablespoons water
- Small bowl
- One tablespoon food coloring
- One cup vinegar
- Dinosaur models and other props

INSTRUCTIONS

1. Build your volcano by cutting out a small circle from the center of your piece of card, then wrapping the card around the neck of your water bottle and taping it together. Or you could build up a volcano shape around the bottle using papier-mâché.

2. Decorate your volcano with paint. Think about what colors a volcano would be.

3. Create a scene for your volcano. Paint more pieces of card as the ground. Paint grasslands, swamps, or lakes if you like. Add model trees and dinosaurs. What else can you think of?

4. To make your lava, in a measuring jug mix the baking soda, soap, and water. Pour this mixture into the water bottle.

5. In a small bowl, mix together the food coloring and vinegar. Red is best for a lovely lava color.

6. When you're ready, pour the vinegar mixture into the volcano. Watch as it erupts.

THINK ABOUT IT

Life in a fiery, volcanic world was very different to our lives in the modern world. What effects do you think regular volcanic eruptions would have had on the lives of the dinosaurs?

WATCH THIS!

HOW TO MAKE A VOLCANO

SCAN WITH YOUR PHONE OR TABLET
https://bit.ly/38E6CkL

SCAN HERE!

HOW TO MAKE PAPIER-MÂCHÉ

SCAN WITH YOUR PHONE OR TABLET
https://bit.ly/3ulPgkS

©2023 by Future Publishing Limited

Articles in this issue are translated or reproduced from *Future Genius: Dinosaurs* and are the copyright of or licensed to Future Publishing Limited, a Future plc group company, UK 2022.

Used under license. All rights reserved. This version published by Fox Chapel Publishing Company, Inc., 903 Square Street, Mount Joy, PA 17552.

ISBN 978-1-64124-312-4

Library of Congress Cataloging-in-Publication Data

To learn more about the other great books from Fox Chapel Publishing, or to find a retailer near you, call toll-free 800-457-9112 or visit us at www.FoxChapelPublishing.com.

We are always looking for talented authors. To submit an idea, please send a brief inquiry to acquisitions@foxchapelpublishing.com.

Printed in China
First printing